The American Bar Association
ABA-CLE Career Resource Center
Presents

CONSTRUCTING CORE COMPETENCIES

Using Competency Models to Manage Firm Talent

By
Heather Bock, Ph.D.
with an Introduction by
Robert Ruyak, J.D.,
Chairman and CEO of Howrey LLP

Defending Liberty
Pursuing Justice

The materials contained herein represent the opinions of the authors and editors and should not be construed to be the action of the American Bar Association, the Center for Continuing Legal Education, or Career Resource Center unless adopted pursuant to the bylaws of the Association.

Nothing contained in this book is to be considered as the rendering of legal advice for specific cases, and readers are responsible for obtaining such advice from their own legal counsel. This book and any forms and agreements herein are intended for educational and informational purposes only.

© 2006 by the American Bar Association. All right reserved.

No part of the publication may be reproduced, stored in a retrieval system, or transmitted in any form or by any means, electronic, mechanical, photocopying, recording, or otherwise, without the prior written permission of the publisher. Permission requests should be sent to the American Bar Association Copyrights & Contracts Department via e-mail at copyright@abanet.org or via fax at 312.988.6030.

Printed in the United States of America.

ISBN-10: 1-59031-491-3
ISBN-13: 978-1-59031-491-3

This publication was produced by the American Bar Association ABA-CLE Career Resource Center.

Competency material on pages 14-19 and the illustration of the Howrey U Campus on page 52 were provided courtesy of Howrey LLP and are reprinted with permission. © Howrey LLP. All rights reserved.

About the Authors and Their Firm

Robert F. Ruyak, J.D., is Howrey's Chairman and CEO, and serves as chair of the firm's Executive Committee. He is one of the firm's most experienced and successful trial lawyers. A partner at Howrey since 1981, Ruyak has extensive litigation and jury trial experience covering a wide range of commercial disputes and substantive areas of law. He has tried cases in the antitrust, patent, trade secret, insurance coverage, commercial contract, and international trade areas. His experience encompasses matters involving computer hardware, software, semiconductors, telecommunications, medical devices, chemicals, food, steel, paper, transportation, heavy equipment, and automobiles, among others. He specializes in managing and trying complex cases, representing plaintiffs as well as defendants. Ruyak received his B.A. from Gannon University in 1971 and his J.D. from Georgetown University Law Center in 1974. He then clerked for the Honorable John J. Sirica, United States District Court for the District of Columbia. Ruyak has been admitted to the bar in Pennsylvania (1974) and the District of Columbia (1976), as well as to the United States Courts of Appeals for the District of Columbia, Third, Fourth, Fifth, and Federal Circuits and the United States Supreme Court.

Heather Bock, Ph.D., is the Director of Professional Development for Howrey LLP. She facilitates learning and development initiatives across the firm for attorneys. Prior to joining Howrey, she was the Director of Organizational Effectiveness at AOL Time Warner. Her other work experience includes designing programs and delivering training at Andersen's international training center and consulting to Fortune 500 companies on HR strategy, organizational transformation, and culture change, and diversity. Prior to this, she was adjunct faculty at the Business School at The University of North Carolina at Chapel Hill.

Introduction

The verb *innovate* is most often defined as "to create a new method of performing an ordinary task." In a profession that tends to be "old school" and traditionally as risk averse as they come, developing and implementing new solutions to old problems often requires a healthy dose of vision, planning, and good old arm twisting. This book, written by our colleagues at Howrey, is designed to help firms who want to look beyond the conventional approaches to building their overall law business and explore new ways to serve clients and their business objectives, proactively rather than reactively.

The uninitiated often mistakenly believe that a business development plan is only about bringing more billable cases or projects into the firm. Equally important, however, to this external objective, are the internal aspects of the business plan. A successful plan must address the internal direction of the firm. Most obvious are things like the firm's implementation of technology, support services, and financial controls. Perhaps not so obvious are elements that impact the life of a law firm, including its people, their professional development, and their personal growth.

Somewhere along the line in our planning process we were confronted with the realization that this latter aspect, a detailed plan and approach to the personal and professional development of human assets, is absolutely critical to success. Innovation is essential; the old methods do not serve us well. This is particularly true as you attempt to manage your associate staff—a group of extremely intelligent, highly motivated, evolving professionals, capable of rapid growth, if such growth is properly fueled.

What we describe in this book is one innovative option, which is fueling such development within our firm. It is comprised of several elements: (1) a "Competency Model," (2) a progressive professional development management program engineered to complement it, and (3) a redefined culture and structure to support it.

Restructuring a firm's professional development program will likely require the creation of a comprehensive system and structure for defining associate job performance (a "competency model")—something more prevalent in the corporate work world but, thus far, foreign to law firms. This model must then be implemented and relied upon as a measuring device when conducting performance evaluations and recruiting talent. It also should serve as the objective skills and experience template for the design of essential educational and training programs. Of course, professional evaluation and development should not stop at the associate ranks. Partners, historically and currently, seldom receive systematic or consistent support in furtherance of their career development, yet they are the stars who ensure that the firm's clients are well represented and satisfied.

In addition, competency models will, of necessity, differ by firm and practice (corporate transactions vs. litigation, for example), which may require broad-based firms to have two or more. Sound too complicated? It's really not. It's something that your firm can do. We did. All it takes is a strong focus on your firm's goals and a team of people willing to help execute change within your culture. It also requires leadership, courage, time, and a little money.

As we look ahead, talent management will become an increasingly important competitive advantage for law firms. The ability to adapt to the needs of each generation of associates and partners will have a decided impact on your firm's ability to recruit, retain, and develop the best talent. There are "best practices" and lessons to be learned from Corporate America's approach to talent management by thinking of your attorneys as customers and creating a value proposition that makes them want to remain a part of and succeed at your firm. If you do, you will help your attorneys align their personal and career goals with the firm's strategic plan and have a more productive and engaged workforce.

At Howrey, we know we have much more to do as we continue the process of aligning our competency model with our culture. We think you'll agree that the efforts are worth it. And we hope that the practical advice we offer here, along with our experiences, will inspire your firm to accept the challenge of creating your own innovative approach to talent management and development. It's truly worth it.

Robert Ruyak
September 2005

A Note to Professional Development Staff

As firms recognize the importance of professional development, they may consider bringing in corporate talent to implement change.

In order to define and then provide and benchmark the skills our associates needed to thrive, the Training and Professional Development Committee and I began developing the competency model in 2003, shortly after I joined Howrey. I had competency modeling experience, but not in a law firm setting. I was able to articulate the benefits of creating an organization-wide culture based on those experiences, and the Training and Professional Development Committee, which was looking for a way to respond to the need for an increase in the rigor applied to associate development as well as the need for a systematic approach, found the idea appealing. By partnering with the committee's chair, Martin Cunniff, we were able to introduce the concept to the firm's key committee chairs and partners quickly, and gain support for designing a unique competency model for the firm.

We developed a business case and plan for building a Howrey-centric competency model to present to the Executive Committee. When Robert Ruyak, our firm's managing partner, reviewed the plan and began to understand the firm-wide implications, he made it a priority at the 2004 annual partners' meeting and became a prominent champion for building the model. And as a result, we were off and running.

Next, we assembled four expert panels comprised of partners on the Performance Evaluation and Training and Professional Development Committees from every office, and we also conducted several associate panels. Each panel met for one two-hour meeting facilitated by a consultant or me. Attorneys worked in groups, reading, discussing, and writing competencies they thought were critical to the job, as well as descriptions of the competencies at both the basic and mastery levels. Each group's comments were then consolidated and circulated to the next expert panel. Ultimately, one out of every four attorneys at the firm "touched" the competency document.

We also communicated often to get everyone involved. We identified our primary stakeholders as the managing partner, the Executive Committee, all partners, local office leadership, the Training and Professional Development Committee, the Performance Evaluation Committee, representatives of the Associate Affairs Committee, and focus group participants.

I worked closely with the chairs of the Training and Performance Evaluation Committees to communicate the competency model to all of the offices. It was this level of partner involvement for rollout of the model that was critical and demonstrated sponsorship by firm leaders.

At the time of this writing, our associates are still adjusting to the competency model and its integration into associate development. Our hope is that having a uniform model will increase associates' career success and our client service.

Heather Bock
September 2005

Table of Contents

■　■　■

Chapter

1

A New Path to Partner: The Competency Model

What happens when a law firm decides it can increase the level of its overall performance by changing the way it hires, evaluates, and trains its associates? What happens when it decides to incorporate a page from Corporate America to contribute to the process?

. Professional development in law firms is a serious—and changing—business. The old evaluation, training, and hiring methods are no longer effective, and many firms are turning to established management programs found in American businesses for solutions to their professional development problems. One such method being explored is the competency model, a hot topic among professional development leaders in law firms.

There are many steps to building a competency model for attorneys, with just as many for making the model "stick." It might seem an easy task for a law firm to come up with a list of competencies that apply to its attorneys, but without adding additional elements to the program, your firm or legal department may not find it as helpful as intended.

If you are considering implementing a competency model at your workplace, keep these key questions in mind:

- Are the competencies you articulate the ones that are going to make the firm successful in the future?
- Does the model include both hard (technical) skills (such as factual investigation) and soft skills (such as client development and team work)?
- Does the thinking behind the competency model reflect the thinking and practices of the leadership and attorneys across the law firm?
- Is there buy-in and support for the final program?
- Will the program be embraced and integrated into the firm's administrative committees?
- How will you measure success?

This book outlines the key issues and principles that you can follow when creating and implementing a competency model in order to maximize its benefit. We will share the methods you can use to create your firm's competency model, along with the reactions of our partners and associates and the overall impact of our model. We also will share our lessons learned so that you might improve upon our process.

Overview of the Law Firm Professional Development Landscape

Professional development in the legal area has changed over the last ten years. According to Ida Abbott, author of *Lawyers' Professional Development: The Legal Employer's Comprehensive Guide*, billable hours have become the primary focus for most attorneys working in law firms today. The emphasis on billing as many hours as possible has not left much time or incentive for working toward developing one's career. Individual attorneys have the personal desire, but often lack the time or know-how to do career planning. Combined with the consolidation of firms and high turnover rates, firms are discovering a serious need for positive reorganization and commitment to providing development opportunities wherever they can. Abbott sees this as a positive development for the professional development area in general.

"Firms need to create strategic management plans that allow individuals to create their own professional development plans, which should mesh with the overall goals of the business," Abbott said. "Look at the systems your firm uses: Do these systems for getting work done support professional development? Are these systems integrated with one another? How does your firm make assignments?" Answering these questions in light of your firm's overall business strategy will help you create the systems and programs you need to support your attorneys.

"It is important that associates determine what it means to be 'professional'—and this means providing service beyond billing hours," Abbott said. "They also need to view their careers as reaching past the immediate task—what kinds of attorneys do they really want to be?" In addition, written competencies help associates address these questions.

Abbott has found that firms are beginning to incorporate competency models into their professional development and training plans, as well as into their performance evaluation systems. She thinks these efforts are positive steps, but warns that firms must be careful not to let their lists of competencies take on a life of their own. Rather than becoming mere checklists that define jobs or enumerate areas in which an attorney must master for promotion, competency models must be integrated into the overall cultures of the firms, and tying training to competencies is a unique approach.

Competency Model Background

Although competency models have been around for more than 20 years to evaluate employees, define job performance, and determine compensation, they are just making a debut in law firms.

In 1982, organizational behavior author and consultant R.E. Boyatzis defined *competency* as "an underlying characteristic of an individual which is causally related to effective or superior performance in a job. Competencies can be motives, traits, self-concepts, attitudes or values, content knowledge, or cognitive or behavioral skills—any individual characteristic that can be measured or counted reliably and that can be shown to differentiate significantly between superior and average performers, or between effective and ineffective performers." Boyatzis defined differentiating competencies as those that could distinguish superior performers from those who were average, and threshold competencies as those that defined adequate job performance. Competency programs became recognized means that work to take the subjective focus out of what should be objective employee evaluations.

A competency model is a customized list of behaviors and skills used to distinguish or predict employee performance within a business. In a law firm, the model defines various behaviors and skills—and the developmental levels of those behaviors and skills—that are necessary as each attorney progresses on the path to partner. Competency models can be tailored to reflect a business's individual strategy and vision. Effective integration of a competency model can enable the business to better achieve its long-term strategic objectives, and create or enhance a high-performance learning culture.

For a law firm, where the "product" is the knowledge and skills of its attorneys, a productive culture is one in which attorneys:

- Are fully engaged in their work;
- Are operating at maximum professional skill level; and
- Have the resources available to regularly and consistently improve those skills.

True, the core competencies and related components that work for one firm may not be successful at your firm—after all, what makes firms competitively distinguishable must be preserved. However, the foundation for and the process of building a competency model is similar for any firm that wants to incorporate it into its professional development program. For example, most firms will find that focusing on junior attorney skill development needs to be a priority because it will improve the firm's overall professional talent pool, and help leverage that pool across the enterprise.

New attorneys' raw professional talents need to be refined in order to sell them to clients. An inadequately trained associate may not have the skills or experiences to properly depose an expert witness, but with a competency model in place that identifies this as a crucial skill area, the training can be designed to enable him or her to practice this skill and appropriately conduct a deposition. In addition, he or she will probably also develop the foundational understanding regarding recovery when a deponent's answers go awry.

Using Competency Models to Create a High-Performance Culture

In sum, in order to create a high-performing culture, a firm must consistently encourage and provide resources to its attorneys to build professional skills. By identifying critical competencies, professional development tactics (such as training, assignments, and pro bono cases) will target the specific skills associates need. Providing these development opportunities will allow the firm to offer an increasingly better "product" to its clients.

Competency Insights from Others in the Field

Firms across the country are contemplating refined professional development programs that use core competencies as a foundation. Many have explored competency models, and some have implemented them while others have opted to go in a different direction. Here are the insights from three other firms, one in-house counsel, and our own firm regarding competency systems on why they would or would not create a competency model.

Seyfarth Shaw, LLP

Seyfarth Shaw, LLP in Chicago has recently implemented a competency model to enhance its professional development program. Judy Braun, Chief Development Officer, came to the firm from a medical device company that had successfully used a competency model to define job performance. Braun was able to quickly discern that the firm's performance management system was in need of improvement, as was its general use of feedback and coaching. She says that Seyfarth associates received some feedback on their writing skills, but not on other important dimensions of the job, like business development or client management skills. Further, firm coaching was inconsistent and often unhelpful. Associates were frustrated and confused about what was expected of them, and morale continued to be an issue.

       Braun, like many transplants from the corporate world, recognized the need for a business-like approach to professional development and identified the competency model as a strategic method for defining and evaluating associate performance at her firm. With the new system in place, Braun said that partners and associates are pleased with the program and morale has improved. Now, expectations are clear and consistent, coaching and feedback are more regular, and rewards are aligned with the competencies. It's an integrated development system.

"Creating a program like this is a journey," Braun said, and she agrees that it is one worth taking.

Arnold & Porter LLP

Caren Ulrich Stacy, Director of Professional Development and Legal Personnel at the Washington, D.C., firm of Arnold & Porter LLP, points out some of the challenges associated with creating a competency model. As you work to enhance your professional development programs, you not only need to be aware of the positive aspects of creating a competency model, but you must be fully cognizant of the amount of time, money, and continued effort such a program will entail.

Stacy agrees that core competency lists are often helpful guides for developing training plans, and they can serve as useful roadmaps for associates. But, she warns, there are several significant challenges—and possible downsides—to developing, administering, and updating these lists.

"First and foremost, it takes time to develop accurate and comprehensive competency lists. Lawyers in the firm, typically partners, must spend countless hours drafting lists and obtaining buy-in from the other members of the partnership to ensure that the competencies accurately represent the necessary skills lawyers in the firm need to embody to advance and succeed. In law firms lacking sufficient professional personnel or attorneys who have the time necessary to commit to the process, expensive consultants are often hired to assist in this process. Whether done in-house or with outside expertise, costs can reach into the thousands. And then, to be sure the competencies stay current and move with business, market, and economic trends of the industry and the world, they need to be updated periodically. Similar to strategic plans, these competency lists must serve as living documents in order to remain valuable on an ongoing basis. If you neglect to update them, much of your time, energy, and money spent creating them will be wasted."

Another possible challenge is implementation. Before the competencies are put into practice, law firm management must answer several important questions that often involve high-level policy decisions. In collaboration with these decisions, foundational systems typically need to be refined, or created in some instances, to support the use of the competency lists.

Questions to ask to determine whether your firm should embark on a competency building process include:

- Will the core competency models be connected to annual evaluations?
- How will the firm support the associates' ability to gain the skills on the lists?
- How will associates be fairly evaluated on their performance?
- Will the firm establish a work-coordination system to ensure that assignments are distributed equally so that all associates have the necessary experience to be competent in an area?

Without the proper guidelines and expectations regarding work assignments, training, and performance reviews, associates can often mistake core competency lists as employment contracts. An associate may expect that the law firm will supply him or her with the training or support to acquire the skills on the competency list and anticipate that if each of the skills is mastered, he or she will automatically advance to partnership. This is a crucial point that must be clearly explained to everyone involved in the creation of your model.

"Before undertaking the arduous process of establishing, administering, and updating core competency lists, firms should weigh their specific needs against the possible downsides and entertain other options accordingly," commented Stacy.

For instance, a training curriculum can be designed and developed though means such as needs assessment interviews with the attorneys, firm-wide surveys, committee and focus group assistance, management discussions regarding firm strategy and business goals, feedback from clients, and examination of attorney performance reviews and upward evaluations. These methods provide a similar end product to core competency lists—the critical skills and subsequent training plans that lawyers need to become the best legal counsel and advocates for their clients.

Nixon Peabody LLP

Christine White, firm-wide director of professional personnel at Nixon Peabody LLP in Washington, D.C., is taking a methodical and measured approach to evaluating the need for a competency model at her firm. The firm's current well-developed program already offers more than 140 trainings annually and uses a formal evaluation process and outside training resources to support associate professional growth.

"Based on my experience at four law firms and as a consultant, there are two keys to success," said White. "One is to manage expectations, and the second is to create systems and programs that support career management. Firms that understand 'career management' understand the links that connect all facets of an associate's life—what I call 'pathways.' I have found that it is critical to have consistent career management messages starting with the first pathway, the employment interview, and continuing through the other pathways of orientation, mentoring, evaluation and feedback, work assignment decisions, and training."

An In-House Perspective

Suki Dicker is associate general counsel for BAE Systems, Inc. A transplant from a magic circle law firm in the United Kingdom, she joined BAE Systems plc in 1997 and transferred to the U.S. operation (BAE Systems, Inc.) in 2001.

Dicker calls herself a "great supporter of learning and development in law firms." "One of the attractions of joining a UK magic circle firm is the ability to build skills," said Dicker. "There appears to be a much greater emphasis in UK law firms on training and development than there is here in the United States. I am surprised at how under-developed the training and development function is in most U.S. law firms, how it is not generally seen as a key to success."

Dicker is very positive about the benefits a comprehensive training and development program can bring to her both as a law firm client and as a member of a 30-attorney in-house legal function. She said that when she knows a firm she is working with has a solid training program that includes a competency model, she can be more confident that its associates have received appropriate and relevant training and are capable of performing the job she is asking them to perform. It also helps in ensuring that quality and skill sets are consistent across a class of associates.

"Too often in law firms, even top-drawer firms, the quality of associates and even partners can be patchy," Dicker explained. "For a client, this is frustrating."

With the growth of global and large national practices, clients are even more conscious of the need for consistent quality, skill sets, and a global culture. "I want to know that I can get the same quality service from a local office as I can from the firm's headquarters," she said. "Increasingly, I am relying on global practices to service our mergers and acquisitions function. I have more confidence knowing that I will get consistent quality when I know a firm is investing in training and development for all its associates, whether in Europe or the United States."

Dicker also knows that her company's work won't always be used as a training ground for green associates. "Although I accept that part of an associate's training will be on-the-job, I don't want to pay top dollar to teach," she said.

"I like working with happy, healthy associates," Dicker added. "I can see that comprehensive training programs incorporating competency models help to ensure that firms are able to identify a success profile for their attorneys, that the attorneys are developing consistent skills, and that they are confident in those skills. This is much more effective in terms of the client/law firm relationship than working with associates who are overwhelmed, overworked, and who don't understand enough about what they're doing. Competency models are good ways to manage and develop talent."

BAE Systems has a 10-year-old competency model in place that applies to its senior employees. However, it focuses only on soft skills such as customer service and team work. Dicker appreciates the value these competencies bring to the corporation in terms of cultural and behavioral change, but also notes that there is a definite need for a competency model focusing on technical skills as they relate to the legal function. "It is important that opportunities are provided to young in-house attorneys to show them what success looks like," she said. "They need a framework for the skills they're learning and all of us need the ability to gauge how we are doing and where we can improve. Competency models do both these things."

Howrey LLP

Howrey's decision to create a competency model hinged on its need to maintain its competitive edge by providing clear direction for its associates. Martin Cunniff, chair of the firm's Training and Professional Development Committee, says that life before the model was frustrating—even for management. It was difficult to define what associates should be trained to do, and even more difficult to evaluate associates' skills objectively. The model cleared up inconsistencies in training and helped partners clearly articulate the skills associates needed to develop. The firm uses its model as a foundation for training, recruiting, and performance evaluations.

Howrey's competency model involves the whole firm, and so did its development: the process to develop its model ultimately included input from 25 percent of its attorneys. The result is an attorney competency model that includes 16 competencies—skills, abilities, and behaviors that differentiate levels of superior attorney performance—necessary for success in the junior associate through level one partner roles.

To Create or Not Create a Competency Model: That Is the Question

Reasons to Create a Model:

- *To help your firm develop useful and effective training plans.* A competency model can help your firm consider the nexus between the training offered and its attorneys' articulated wants and needs.

- *To define firm expectations, particularly for associates.* One of the motivations for adopting competencies is to demystify your firm's definition of success. Specifically, core competency lists can become useful roadmaps for associates.

    Rick Ripley, former chair of Howrey's Recruiting and Associate Development Committees, and Joanne Caruso, co-chair of its Attorney Development Committee, supported the firm's competency model because they thought it would be most helpful in managing associate expectations. Ripley, who started as a young associate at the firm, said the evaluation process as it existed before the inception of a competency model did not go deep enough. "Partners filled out forms and ranked associates. The forms were discussed by the Performance Evaluation Committee and the committee talked to the associates: 'Things are going great; do you have any questions?'" He noted that "this generation of associates has higher expectations. They want a delineation of measurement in terms of how they're doing at the firm. They want to know the necessary prescription for success at the firm. The competency model responds to these needs."

    Caruso, who joined the firm as a summer associate and is now the managing partner of Howrey's southern California office, agrees. "The competency model is a thorough and objective evaluation system that helps everyone. It helps the partners know exactly what training is needed so we can provide training that is targeted to develop those specific skills. It also helps associates know exactly what skills they will be evaluated on after the training program has concluded."

- *To create a business-like approach to professional development.* Rather than leaving performance evaluations up to the individual styles of the evaluating partners, a competency model assures associates that everyone is being evaluated in the same way, by the same criteria, based on the business needs of the firm. And, as Howrey's Chief Operating Officer Robert Koenen noted, "A solid training program gives a corporation a competitive advantage." Prior to the implementation of a model, he explained, the firm "had not focused its training to align with its business objectives and the desired career development of its attorneys."

- *To improve feedback quality.* Ed Han, chair of Howrey's Performance Evaluation Committee, defines a competency model as "a rigorously developed concept of what it takes for an associate to become a successful partner. In terms of evaluation, the goal is to capture more specifics about associates' work product and skill sets."
- *To improve training and feedback consistency.* A competency program will help manage training from practice group to practice group, office to office, and partner to partner. Additionally, it will become the foundation for consistency in articulated skills.
- *To improve morale.* Creating a common language that will be used throughout your firm for evaluations and training will improve morale, because everyone will understand the process in the same way. "Having a competency model will improve retention and make our associates better at developing their own careers," Cunniff said.

Reasons Not to Create a Competency Model:

- *Success may hinge on proper in-house talent.* You need the right people on your team in order to develop a viable competency model. You might find that going outside the firm and hiring a non-attorney—someone with corporate development experience—is a good solution.
- *No management interest.* Even after presenting the business case for the effort, management may not be enthusiastic about making significant changes. Your firm culture simply may not be ready to take on this kind of initiative.
- *You can address issues by more efficient (think: less time and money) means.* Tightening up your training process, providing more structure for your mentoring programs, or revising your performance evaluation forms may be all you need to do to help your firm maximize its business strategy and provide direction to your associates.
- *Inability to maintain the competencies.* Carefully evaluate the amount of time and money you have available to devote to the upkeep of your competencies to your firm strategy. If the strategy changes, associate competencies also may have to change to ensure their alignment with firm strategy.

Keys to Competency Success:

- *Manage expectations.* Competency models must be integrated into the overall culture of the firm, and within acceptable parameters. Be sure that everyone understands why you've created your competency model, and be able to demonstrate clearly how the competencies are tied to evaluations and training. Your competency list should in no way be construed as an employment contract or partnership guarantee.

- *Create systems that support career management.* Although a competency model and its related training and evaluation programs may provide associates with direction and guidance as they traverse the road to partner, attorneys still need to take responsibility for their individual career management. Robert Lytle, former chair of Howrey's Associate Affairs Committee, explained, "Associates need to understand that they should continually strive to improve their skills and become better lawyers each day. They need to catch the vision and participate."

In Summary

A customized competency model will become the strategic compass for managing an organization's talent. This is especially critical in professional service firms where skills and knowledge are what differentiate one firm from another in the marketplace.

Before taking on this endeavor, you must perform your due diligence, as you would before taking on any new initiative. Specifically:

- *Talk to people in professional services firms and find out what their experiences have been in developing—or not—competency models.* Many firms use the language of competency models but have not in fact developed a rigorous leveled approach with firm-wide buy-in.
- *Read the professional literature outside of the legal industry for ideas.*
- *Consider the business costs of developing such a program to see if the resources and effort you expend will result in a strong return on investment.* Developing a new professional development program of any sort is an enormous proposition, and you must be sure that you and your firm are ready for the changes it will bring.

Establishing the specific skills associates need to become successful attorneys and potential future partners in a multifaceted firm is an enormous undertaking. With the help of partners, associates, and possibly outside consultants, you can develop a list that clearly defines the skills your firm attorneys need to be successful.

The Move to a Competency Model

It's no secret that the economy can unilaterally change the way business is done and affect not only corporations but the service industry as well. For example, law firms, even the large ones, were affected as fundamentally as everyone else when the post-Internet bubble burst in the 1990s. During that time, corporate clients not only downsized internally, but also began to downsize in terms of the number of law firms they retained annually. Moreover, these clients began to expect their attorneys to be as business savvy as they were. It became clear that attorneys in law firms were going to have to become less insular and ready to compete in order to maintain a competitive edge in the new marketplace. It became even more important under these circumstances to retain associates after spending thousands of training and recruiting dollars on them.

Associates changed, too. First-year associates were more tech-savvy than ever before. They wanted clear definitions of the firm's expectations for their professional development. They wanted to know specifically what they were supposed to do to be successful in the firm. They wanted to achieve a "better" work/life balance. They wanted to pay off their college loans, but didn't want to kill themselves doing it, and they knew they didn't have to. The competition for talent was so fierce among large, new millennium law firms that associate salaries increased exorbitantly, reaching well beyond the $100,000 mark. Firm recruiting and training dollars were stretched farther than ever.

During that time, the question became: How can a firm balance its business needs with the needs of these new associates and still remain competitive and cutting edge?

Developing a competency model helps build a value proposition for associates. It shows the firm's commitment to making associate advancement more transparent by outlining what its partners think are critical competencies for success. It also allows them to build their skills proactively, since they now have explicit definitions and examples of behaviors to focus on and master.

The drivers of the competency model can come from many directions—both internal and external.

First Steps

If you determine that a core competency model is something your firm should pursue, these steps will help you bring the model to life.

1. Enlist outside experts for assistance in developing and implementing your competency model. If you are a global firm, seek out a consulting firm focused on global organizational and/or human resources. Keep in mind, however, that partnering with a group that hasn't worked with a law firm before is somewhat of a mixed blessing. For example, many of the soft skills (e.g., leadership and project management) you identify as important competencies are ones that the consultant has likely helped other professional services firms develop, but there may be a steep learning curve when it comes to helping you identify and define the core technical legal skills—the hard skills—you also need to incorporate into your model. This is where your partners come in.

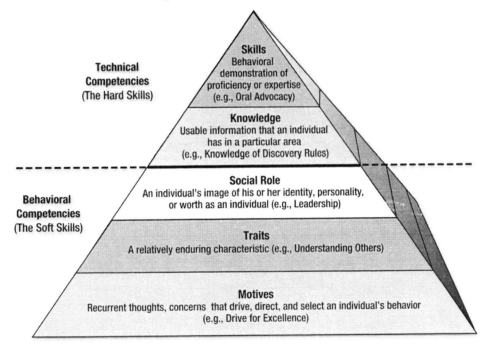

The foundational skills outlined by a competency model build on one another. The soft skills define the behavior of an individual and create the foundation that supports the hard skills. Without motives, traits, and social roles, the technical competencies—knowledge and skills—have no context.

Lori Berman, Ph.D., manager, Professional Development, who worked as an outside consultant in developing Howrey's competency model, explains that the primary distinction among organizations is technical skills.

"We see the same behavioral competencies or skill sets coming up again and again—competencies like leadership, teamwork, impact and influence, customer service orientation, the drive for excellence, and self growth. It is the technical competencies that are most unique to specific businesses. In the case of law firms, these include the skills associated specifically with the practice of law: taking and defending depositions, factual investigation, etc."

Partner involvement is the final key to success in translating the potential value of building a competency model.

In a competency model, each competency should relate to a specific group of skills, and these skills should be broken into developmental levels. However, these developmental levels do not have to correspond to the levels associates occupy at the firm. In other words, it is not necessary to articulate specific competencies in which third-year associates are expected to be proficient. Rather, allowing each competency level to build on the one before it, along with the individual's own professional development plan and his or her work experience, can determine when a specific competency is mastered. For example, a first-year associate may be at level 2 of the negotiation skills competency, but only at level 1 of the written advocacy section of the same competency. Having this higher level of mastery in one area allows the associate to concentrate on the area he or she has not yet mastered, which will ultimately strengthen his or her position in the overall competency.

As you refine your own competency model and gather more detailed information about associates' performance, you may consider more closely aligning the competency levels with associate levels.

Overall, the competencies need to align with firm strategy. For example, Howrey's competencies cover the following areas of attorney development:

- Building the Case for the Client

    o Legal Research and Analysis
    o Factual Development and Investigation
    o Mastery of Substantive and Procedural Law
    o Creative Problem Solving

- Advocating for the Client
  - o Written Advocacy
  - o Oral Advocacy
  - o Negotiation Skills
  - o Trial and Courtroom Skills

- Working with Others
  - o Project/Case Management
  - o Leadership
  - o Working Cooperatively and Effectively with Others
  - o Internal Communication and Support

- Positioning Self and Firm for Success
  - o Client Service and Communication
  - o Drive for Excellence
  - o Growing the Business
  - o Developing Self

©Howrey LLP

2. Develop competencies based on input from partners and associates across offices and practice areas. Solicit input regarding the skills, abilities, and behaviors considered the most important to achieve superior performance at your firm. One challenge for law firms, particularly the larger ones, in developing a model may be making it applicable and useful in various practice areas and office locations. Remember to keep it flexible enough to apply to varying jurisdictions and their individual processes. You can always drill down on the practice-specific competencies in a later phase of development.

3. *Use your resulting model to pave the way for a new professional development curriculum for associates.* Consider incorporating online programs, training academies, and partners who are willing to serve as firm-wide resources (we call ours "competency czars"). You also may want to revise your performance evaluation systems, as well as the tactics for linking assignments and pro bono work with professional development opportunities. We'll go into more detail on this area in Chapter 3.

Changing the culture of an organization is a difficult task under the best circumstances, and when the decision is made to fiddle with core institutions like evaluations and hiring, this change must be managed carefully. Planning is crucial; communication is essential. In the upcoming chapters, we'll explore how to create and implement a competency model, as well as how the workplace culture may change as a result.

Two Example Competencies

Competencies should include skills, abilities, and behaviors—both hard and soft—that differentiate levels of performance in an attorney's job. Each one should relate to an area of performance. The following example competency is specifically related to litigation, a hard skill. Competencies and corresponding levels should vary by the needs of the law firm implementing them.

Factual Development and Investigation Competency

This competency includes the ability to collect, develop, and organize documents and other information in a coherent fashion for use in factual analyses, additional information gathering, interviewing, and depositions. It involves tenacity and creativity in terms of potential sources of information and getting others to disclose needed information. These skills are used in discovery processes, investigations, second request responses, or similar processes.

Competency Levels

Level 1: Preparation and Support

- Uses all available sources of information.
- Recognizes the primary and critical importance of facts.
- Efficiently and accurately reviews documents for privilege and relevance.
- Prepares sufficient and accurate discovery responses and/or supporting declarations.
- Effectively supports others in preparing for interviews and depositions, identifying relevant documents to review with witnesses, and assembling draft questions and outlines in an effective and user-friendly manner.
- Elicits information about sources of facts, witnesses, data, and documents (e.g., calls employees at client to find documents and individuals with relevant information about the case/issue).
- Assists in witness preparation.

Level 2: Effective Execution

- Thoroughly investigates, develops, and organizes factual records in an advantageous manner.
- Prepares discovery responses and supporting declarations in an insightful fashion.
- Effectively prepares discovery requests based on appropriate consultation with the client and experts.
- Analyzes responses to discovery requests, takes appropriate action to monitor compliance, and documents lack of compliance with the request.
- Manages document productions, second request responses, and similar processes in an efficient and advantageous manner, and coordinates such collections with other parties.
- Conducts proficient interviews/depositions to obtain helpful/necessary information from "non-critical" witnesses.
- Thoroughly prepares witnesses.

Level 3: Factual Tactician-Discovery General

- Investigates, develops, and organizes factual records in a creative and innovative manner.
- Constructs discovery requests and responses (including supporting declarations) to achieve positive results in other phases of litigation or regulatory proceedings.
- Performs all types of interviews/depositions with witnesses of all types (e.g., cooperative, hostile, non-critical, critical, senior, junior).
- Develops plans, themes, and strategies for obtaining and using evidence.
- Positions others to regularly collect and summarize information for him or her.
- Uses consultants' opinions as guides to developing facts.
- Deals effectively with opposing counsel in managing discovery disputes.

© Howrey LLP

Leadership Competency

Leadership is taking an active role in motivating, inspiring, and coaching people to enable team, individual, and organizational effectiveness.

Competency Levels

Level 1: Looks after the Team

- Makes sure the practical needs of the team are met—obtains needed resources, information, personnel, etc.
- Understands the experience and capabilities of team members and works to ensure gaps are filled (e.g., getting the right people).
- Treats all team members with fairness and respect.
- Helps new team members get up to speed.

Level 2: Promotes Team Effectiveness

- Implements well thought-out efforts to enhance team morale and productivity.
- Sets high standards for the team.
- Organizes people and resources toward the effective and efficient pursuit of predetermined objectives.
- Creates an environment that promotes sharing of diverse perspectives and differing viewpoints.
- Communicates team achievements and supports individuals' career objectives.

Level 3: Promotes Individual Effectiveness by Developing Team Members

- Acts as a performance coach by providing tools and giving practical support to others when learning how to approach a task or problem, and communicates the underlying rationale so others can think through future issues on their own.
- Based on an objective assessment of an individual's strengths and areas for development, gives specific feedback to develop and motivate the individual.
- Gives negative feedback in behavioral rather than personal terms.

Level 4: Acts as Steward of the Firm

- Thinks beyond present responsibilities and invests in the firm by actively participating as a leader in firm initiatives or management activities (e.g., firm governance, committees, etc.). In doing so, efficiently uses time for the good of the firm.
- Channels ambition into the firm, not self.
- Displays ingenuity in meeting challenges combined with a care for people.

Level 5: Communicates a Compelling Vision

- Stimulates the group to higher performance standards.
- Generates excitement and commitment to the vigorous pursuit of a clear and compelling vision.
- Drives the vision *and* objectives based on rationale and expertise, not positional power.
- Drives execution and implementation of the vision.
- Leads with quiet, calm determination.

© Howrey LLP

Chapter

2 From Theory to Reality: Development of the Competency Program

As you explore the possibility of putting a competency program into effect in your organization, it is important to be methodical about every step. In essence, you are proposing to change some very basic elements of your corporate culture. Not everyone you talk to initially will agree with the need to change. Not everyone will be as enthusiastic as you are. But you need the buy-in of *every* person who will be affected. Careful planning and clear communications are the keys to implementing your new program efficiently and effectively.

First Things First

It may seem obvious, but as the old song says, "Let's start at the very beginning." Initiating a competency program has many levels of complexity and you may see several starting points. It is best to start with these three steps:

1. Lay the Groundwork

Before you do anything else, build a clear business case for developing a customized competency model for your firm, and be able to articulate the reasons you need the model. Share this with firm leaders and get their support. The business case should explain why a competency model is going to help retention, promote professional development, enhance client service, or make the firm more competitive.

Your reasons for wanting to develop a competency model will be individual to your firm, and you might find the drivers coming from several different factions of the firm. For example, perhaps your associates are unsure and concerned about their professional development paths. This reason alone can be the primary impetus for building a strategic training and professional development program, and it may lead you to link development to performance evaluations. When you approach partners for input, they may express the need for consistent skill development and the ability to cross-staff matters. This is another excellent reason for developing your competency model. Whatever your reasons, make sure you can express them clearly, concisely, and consistently.

Business Case Checklist

The following items are important as you build your business case for the adoption of your competency model. You'll likely have others to add, but being able to answer these questions will help as you present your initiative to firm management.

✓ *How will the model support the firm's strategy?*
✓ *How will the model improve associate recruitment and retention?*
✓ *What is the value your firm hopes to gain from a competency-driven associate development strategy?*
✓ *How does this new approach fit into the current culture of your firm? How will it improve the culture?*
✓ *How will this model make the firm more competitive for talent and for clients?*
✓ *How will this better leverage partner time?*

---

2. Find Champions

Identify the firm leaders who will be key sponsors of the competency model and utilize them to align firm committees. The managing partner may be the best person to start with, but chairs of training or evaluation committees also may be good sponsors. If you are pioneering this process as a staff person, it is critical to have a well-respected partner be the model's spokesperson. Being effective at initiating change in a law firm is difficult under any circumstances. Staff people need to be especially careful to put ego aside and gain satisfaction from making an impact rather than from getting credit.

3. Explain It

Determine the most basic reason driving the decision to build a firm-wide competency model and create an easy one- or two-minute explanation for why it's good for the firm. Your reasoning for the model should build on the strengths or most urgent business needs in your firm. For example, if being innovative is your firm's strength, your explanation should highlight that developing a competency model is innovative for law firms. If associate morale is down because they don't understand what it takes to be successful or they don't think the evaluation process is fair, your explanation should show how the competency model will be part of the solution.

These three steps will be the foundation of your work to develop and implement a viable competency model in your firm. If you take the time you need to lay this foundation, you will have created a strong base from which to work.

Create a Competency Model—You Can Do It Too

Competencies are helpful for any organization that wants to take a more disciplined approach to identifying the key behaviors and skills its employees need to make the company successful. For professional service firms, especially those that compete in a knowledge-based arena as law firms do, it is a greater challenge to identify essential skills, and an even more monumental task to make sure training is available to build those skills. Law firms know that the process of building and developing associates' skills is critical to the firms' success, and they have employed various strategies to ensure that their associates are trained to their exacting standards and gain the skills necessary to be effective partners.

Using a competency model is not only a strategic way to focus talent, but such a model also can build a strong corporate culture. Employees become familiar with the language used to define the competencies, and eventually the entire organization begins to speak consistently when talking about its employees' professional development goals. Individual competencies can be tailored to your firm's specific needs: some competencies will focus on what needs to be done (investigating facts, negotiating, etc.), and other competencies focus on how that work is accomplished (working effectively with others, managing change, etc.). Clearly defined competencies can improve associate performance. If every associate is better skilled at his or her job, it makes sense to expect that overall firm performance also will improve. As more associates reach superior levels of performance—even in just one or two areas—there comes a tipping point after which the entire organization will become more productive.

As you involve your committees, partners, and associates in the development of your firm's competency model, you will discover that organizational change like this is infectious. As Malcolm Gladwell said in *The Tipping Point: How Little Things Make a Big Difference*, "Ideas and behavior and message and products sometimes behave just like outbreaks of infectious disease," which explains why change often happens quickly once it gets started. A "tipping point" can be likened to the point in an epidemic when the illness reaches critical mass.

Work to create a shared language through the competency model because it will help you reach a tipping point. After using the model for a time, you'll be able to use that language to articulate that the model is connected to the way associate training is described (e.g., Competency A can be mastered through Course X) and integrated into feedback—both formal and informal. In order to do that, you will have to go through the discipline of defining the essential skills your associates need to achieve the firm's business strategy. A set of competencies can become the core foundation into which you integrate all the processes you use to recruit, develop, evaluate, and promote associates. If you align all of these processes, your entire firm's talent will pull in the same direction. You'll then witness, as Gladwell did, that "…behavior can be transmitted from one person to another as easily as the flu or the measles can."

Methodology—How to Create a Competency Model

1. Adapt the Model to Firm Needs

The first thing to remember in developing a competency model is to adapt it to your firm's needs. There is no off-the-shelf solution; every firm is different in terms of its strategic focus, its culture, and its clients. Therefore, each competency model needs to be tailored to suit the firm into which it will be incorporated.

Initially, you must identify and articulate your firm's business strategy and overall vision. Ask several questions:

- What does the firm want to accomplish over the next several years?
- What does the firm need its associates and partners to do to achieve these goals?
- What areas of the law do they need to be proficient in?
- What skills do all attorneys need to accomplish the firm's goals?
- What are the differences in specific practice areas or locations that need special training attention?

As described in Chapter 1, choosing an outside consultant to help facilitate the development of your competency model is important. An outside consultant can add credibility to the process and ensure that it reflects firm-wide input. Once these players are on board and you have answered the above questions, you can move to the next development steps.

2. Identify the Strategic Context for a Competency Model

Next, identify and understand the strategic drivers that enable your firm to compete effectively in its individual marketplace—both its current marketplace and any future areas in which it wants to compete. For example, if your firm wants to be a global litigation firm, its competencies must be tailored to achieve this goal. If your firm wants to be the number one commercial finance player, its competencies must focus on those skills.

3. Define the Organizational Culture of the Firm

When developing your competency program, it is critical to keep in mind the organizational culture of the firm. Every firm has a different culture, and this will impact how well the model is received and how successful it will be in terms of improving the skill base of its associates and achieving the firm's goals.

Furthermore, your firm's culture will dictate the best way to ensure buy-in to your new model. You may find that a particular office or practice area may be critical to firm-wide acceptance. Be sure to involve that group in the design of the initiative. Pay particular attention to how you position the competency model. Specifically, are you using it as a retention tool, as a catalyst for building a training curriculum, or as an enhancement for client service?

Finally, know that your cultural context may influence the development and rollout of your model. For example, determine whether your firm is classified as an early or late adopter of new technologies, systems, or other innovations. This insight may give an indication as to how quickly your firm is willing to create and roll out a model. If you find your firm is a late adopter, do not be frustrated—simply recognize that your firm prefers to see the experience of other law firms before trying a new approach—and use this book to help you state your case. Our firm's early adopter demeanor proved conducive to the competency process—it allowed us to develop a model in six months and roll it out just three months later.

4. Identify Firm Experts

Once you understand your firm's culture—the way work gets done—work next to identify the best group of partners to help you choose which skill sets are critical for success, based on their own experience, vantage points, and strategic firm insights.

Specifically, put together an expert panel of partners and solicit their input. Their overall experience, their knowledge of the firm's goals, and their positions on hiring, training, or evaluation committees naturally gives them a unique perspective on the key success competencies for associates at various stages of development. Your actual competencies will come from these discussions. This panel should reflect various practice areas or offices within the firm—allow for as much diversity and representation as possible at this stage of development. After building your foundational competencies, you also can assemble partner experts to articulate specific competencies that will be appropriate to individual practice areas.

Next, consider insights from those most impacted by the potential model. For example, at our firm, we put together panels of associates from different class years, since they would be the most affected by a competency model and could add good ideas about the skills they feel they need and want to master to become better at what they do. We asked partner panels to review the findings of the associates, and also allowed the associates to review the competencies expressed by the partners.

Once the panels complete their reviews, firm leaders may want to finalize the model and ensure that it is clear, free of inconsistencies, and reflective of the firm's strategic priorities.

5. Conduct Associate Interviews

Competency models may take a variety of forms and various degrees of rigor, depending, as previously mentioned, on the environment in which they are developed. In addition to the input from your expert panels, supplement the information with associate interviews, as they are the ones responsible for delivering on the competencies. Consider using this bottom-up approach in addition to the top-down partner view to ensure that all involved have input into the new system. (This approach additionally shows associates that the firm values not only the hours they bill but also their professional growth.)

Conduct behavioral event interviews with best-in-class associates. This kind of interview is designed to identify the specific behaviors these attorneys display on the job. Rather than simply determining if the interviewee has had a particular experience, a behavioral event interview will reveal exactly how the interviewee managed the experience, both positively and negatively. It is often a good idea to record (audio or video) these interviews so that responses can be measured objectively and specific behaviors identified. It will become clear from these interviews which individuals are superior performers (showing mastery of desired competencies) and which are adequate performers (showing mastery of only the basic skills needed to do the job).

These behaviors can then be reflected in the overall competency model. Once you've identified this list of skills, you can break them down into a list of specific, leveled behaviors. Articulating these layers will give you a set of competencies with three to four performance levels, which ultimately reflect the differences in skill levels between novices and experts. It is important to include insights from the newest associates through the most senior partners in these interviews so that the differences in mastery can be captured.

For example, your attorneys may agree that leadership is an important competency across the board. Thus, you may define leadership in general as "taking an active role in motivating, inspiring, and coaching people to enable team, individual, and organizational effectiveness." Keep in mind that leadership behaviors look different at the novice and expert levels. At the basic level, leadership means looking after the practical needs of the team, and at a more advanced level, leadership means increasing the team's effectiveness through morale building, promoting different perspectives, and communicating well. A high-level leader acts as a steward of the firm and communicates a compelling vision.

Including associate input from all offices and practice areas might help ensure that you create a holistic view of the competencies you want to implement. In our situation, we found that the work sufficiently differed between practice areas; however, we didn't create separate competencies for each. Instead we created a general practice-specific category, which we call "Mastery of Substantive and Procedural Law." We generalized by stating that attorneys need to become knowledgeable within their practice area, whatever that may be.

After setting the foundational competencies, we wanted to have some flexibility and adaptability of our model to leave room for a second phase of development, that of practice-area-specific competencies, which are now in development.

Behavioral Event Interviews Based on Howrey Competencies

What follows is an example of a behavioral event interview. The purpose of this type of interview is to determine not only the experience level of the person being interviewed, but also how the person handled specific situations. The questions are designed to elicit conversation. This interview approach will help you discover more about your interviewees and will help prevent them from telling you what they think you want to hear.

Start the interview with the statement below. (Note: At the beginning of each question, ask the interviewee to start by describing the event in one or two sentences so you will have an idea of what he or she is going to be talking about.)

The purpose of this interview is to learn about you and some of the key experiences of your legal career thus far. I will ask you to talk in detail about some significant work-related events, one at a time. These events should have occurred recently enough for you to talk about them in detail— preferably within the past year or so.

I know that teamwork is often an important aspect of case work; however, for the purpose of this interview we want to find out what your individual involvement was in each particular event or situation. As you describe these events, tell me what actually happened, focusing on your involvement in the situation.

Specifically:

✓ What led up to the situation?
✓ Who was involved?
✓ What did you do and say at the time?
✓ What did you think and feel at the time?
✓ · What was the final outcome of the event or situation?"

Follow-up questions can be used or not, based on how you feel the interview is going and what the person said.

Advocating for the Client: Oral Advocacy

✓ "Tell me about a time when–either one on one or within a group setting—you had to express ideas or opinions so others would understand or be persuaded. This could be in a trial or pre-trial situation, or even in meetings with witnesses or team members."
✓ "What steps did you take in influencing others?"
✓ "How did you determine the tactics you would take?"
✓ "What challenges or obstacles did you face?"
✓ "What was the outcome of your efforts?"

Working with Others: Project/Case Management

✓ "Tell me about a job or project where you had to gather information from many different sources and then create something with the information."
✓ "Tell me about some project management methodologies you have found to be most effective."
✓ "Give me an example of a time when management had to change a plan or approach to which you were committed. How did you feel and how did you explain the change to your team?"
✓ "Tell me about a time when you had to juggle multiple projects."

6. Benchmark

Benchmarking is a useful tool to ensure that you have identified best practices that may not reside in your firm or even within your industry. Many professional service firms, such as consulting and accounting firms, require many of the same behaviors you've likely identified in your competency model (e.g., able to advise clients appropriately and "make rain"). Find out how they measure mastery of these skills and behaviors. Look at the way they define specific skills, and don't be afraid to appropriate those measures. The downside of not benchmarking is that your competencies may be limited solely to the thinking of the people within your organization.

In addition to benchmarking your competency model against other industries, you may work to articulate the competencies in a way that relates to associates' years at the firm. It will take some time and recordkeeping, but being able to benchmark against yourself and your own performance will become one of your most important tools. Over time, you may collect enough data to compare lawyers across associate class years, within and across practice areas, and by office. This will enable you to create a database of evaluations so you can understand variations and expected competency and skill levels for associates in a given year. The intent is not to create a formula for what level of competence an associate has to reach each year of his or her career, but to help partners give management feedback on areas of associate strength and professional development needs.

7. Identify Issues That Don't Fit

Don't be discouraged if you find that there is one practice area or one office or one group where the competency model doesn't fit perfectly. Identifying these "misfitting" issues will help you make the overall model flexible and adaptable.

For example, our firm has international offices, which creates issues revolving around the fact that laws and judicial procedures differ from those in the United States. We asked representatives from our overseas offices to review the model and help apply the essence of the competencies to the attorneys in their locations. Specifically, we asked them to think of each competency in terms of the relevant jurisdiction. Although, for example, the literal insights described within "Factual Development and Investigation" and "Trial and Courtroom Skills" competencies would not apply to European countries that do not have juries or formal discovery processes, the essence of the competency can still be applied, by simply interpreting the concepts through the lens of the European legal system.

8. Put It All Together

We were able to finalize our model, once the expert panels identified the key clusters of competencies that define attorney success, the associate interviews had provided the detail on the behaviors that distinguish the basic and master levels of skills, and the benchmarking informed us of best practices. Again, this is what our leadership needed to see to be comfortable moving forward—your firm may require more, less, and/or different information.

9. Communicate

Regardless of the amount and type of research you determine necessary, communication will prove critical to achieving buy-in and acceptance of your initiative.

The first step is to create a communication plan identifying the following:

- Firm stakeholders;
- Stakeholder concerns and issues;
- Overall communication goals (e.g., awareness, buy-in, commitment of partners to sponsor);
- The appropriate communication vehicle for each of the various participants (committee meeting agendas, videoconferences, e-mail, etc.);
- The appropriate person to send specific messages (managing partner, director of professional development, training chair, local office leadership, etc.); and
- Feedback opportunities.

Create a presentation or communication explaining:

- The purpose of the competency model,
- The process you intend to use for building it, and
- The business case for the initiative.

For example, at our firm, we sent a general e-mail announcement to partners and associates. We asked associate representatives to review and provide feedback on the message before sending it. We then delivered more detailed presentations in person and through videoconferences. We later selected a Training and Performance Evaluation Committee partner to present the information in meetings within each office (see the Toolkit for communication examples). The graphic below showcases the elements our firm used to create its competency model.

Elements for Developing a Competency Model

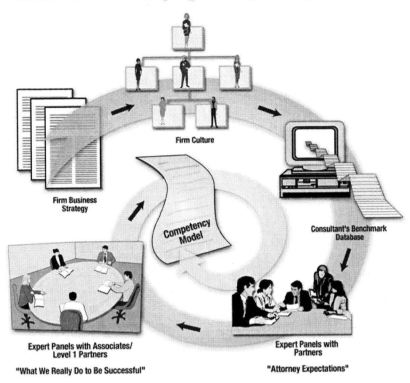

There are many steps to creating a successful competency model, and it all starts with your business strategy. Once you have defined your firm's strategic plan, you can combine the remaining pieces—your culture, input from your consultant, and your expert panels—to create a model that is well suited to your firm.

10. Prioritize Attorney Development

If your firm has been bedeviled by the up-and-out model where attorneys start at the firm, are successful, but then leave after a time, you may benefit from the competency model because it offers your firm an opportunity to place a high value on attorney training and development and correlate it with firm success.

Further, you will show associates they are valuable by asking them for their feedback, revising the model based in part on their insights, and working with them to convert them into champions of the model. Before implementing the model, be sensitive to the fact that it will establish a firm-wide set of professional development expectations for all of your associates. So, for example, if your firm offers both litigation and transactional services, you cannot say that litigation skills are essential for all attorneys regardless of practice area. Once your foundational skills are established, the departments can build on it by creating practice area relevant competencies.

Engaging Committees in the Process

As is typical in law firm management, most firms rely on various committees to handle the administrative aspects of the business. At Howrey, it was helpful that the managing partner not only endorsed the competency model, but also made implementing it a priority. He charged the associate development committees with integrating the model into their committee scope.

When you start to integrate the competency model into the relevant committee(s), these steps may be helpful:

- Identify all the areas in your firm where the competency model should be integrated. If the model is indeed to be the foundation for how attorneys are hired, developed, evaluated, and promoted, it must become the fabric of all those processes. Involve the chairs of the relevant committees early in the process to ensure that they have endorsed the business case for developing a competency model and are invested in making it work.
- Identify a project manager to coordinate the integration, rollout, and change management process. The director or chief learning and development officer is probably the most logical person for this task, but the chief operating officer or another visible committee chair could play the role as well.
- Work with each committee chair (or equivalent) to create a project plan for each committee and include the following components:
  - Committee scope or deliverable (the existing processes to be modified, the end goal)
  - Issues to be addressed by each committee
  - Answers for all the questions associates and partners might ask
  - Development plans
  - Communication plans
  - Implementation and improvement plans

Associate Development Committee Integration

The administrative committees at your firm should be involved in all phases of the development of the competency initiative. Each committee can address several questions in various areas as their participation in the model evolves.

Committee Scope and Key Issues

- ✓ What are the goals of the committee as it relates to the competency model?
- ✓ What existing processes need to be modified?
- ✓ What new processes need to be added?
- ✓ What challenges exist?
- ✓ What opportunities will the competency model create?
- ✓ What is the committee's preliminary action plan?
- ✓ What are the issues this committee needs to address?

Design

- ✓ Determine implications of the competency model on the committee's work.
- ✓ Design new processes based on feedback from key stakeholders.
- ✓ Draft key questions and answers for the frequently asked questions guide for associates.

Training and Professional Development Committee

At Howrey, the Training and Professional Development Committee was the primary driver of the competency initiative.

The committee was aware of the firm's need for a systematic, formalized approach to associate training, and realized that creating firm-wide clarity around what the foundational training needs were was the first hurdle it had to overcome. The committee noticed disparate approaches to training and development in various offices, in part, as a result of firm mergers. Moreover, each office has slightly different expectations in terms of the most important skills, performance expectations at each associate level, and skill development suggestions.

In order to create a comprehensive training curriculum, devising a one-firm understanding of the critical foundational skills became our first goal.

Many associates think career success at their firm is a bit of a black box. Some think success depends on whom they work for rather than what their actual skills are. Others feel there are mixed messages among partners concerning the key career success factors. In multi-office firms, training and development opportunities may even vary by location: some partners proactively offer training, while others are too busy with client work to devote sufficient time to formal training. Part of the goal in developing a competency initiative is to allay these types of concerns.

By developing a firm-wide competency model, you can improve associate development in three key areas:

- Create a common language and focus for giving feedback and coaching to associates when asked, "What am I doing well; what should I do differently?"
- Provide clear behavioral examples of professional development expectations ("I know I'm supposed to be a 'team player,' but what does that mean in terms of how I do my day-to-day work?")
- Develop individual roadmaps for associate advancement or development ("What do I need to do to further my career?")

Mary Craig Calkins, who served on Howrey's Training and Professional Development Committee, credits the model with "creating consistency among the partners. It also reminds associates that the firm is in the service industry." She said the "model gives associates the goals on which they should focus," and believes that the firm will be stronger for having these multifaceted associates.

Next, turn to the balance of your committees to help develop the initiative.

Pro Bono Committee

Generally, a firm's commitment to pro bono work is driven not only by the firm's responsibility to the surrounding community, but also by its commitment to its newest attorneys, since pro bono work offers associates hands-on, real-life experiences early in lawyers' careers. Creating a competency-centric evaluation process allowed our firm to better review attorney assignments on pro bono matters. As associates create and begin working on their personal professional development plans, they can indicate what competencies they want to concentrate on for a period of time. With this information in mind, they can work with the pro bono committee to choose cases that will help them master those competencies.

According to Rachel Strong, a partner who serves on our Pro Bono Committee, there were five attributes of the competency model that convinced the committee that being involved was a good idea:

- The model is central to associate training, particularly through the academies;
- The model will help associates succeed;
- Associates believe the firm is helping them through the investment being made in their futures;
- The model sets the pace so that associates will serve clients better; then clients are satisfied, and the firm is distinguished from other firms; and
- The model attracts better associates.

As the program unfolded, the committee realized that its role was even more important—the committee could narrow the selection of pro bono opportunities to those that met the objectives of the competency model. On occasions when associates request specific kinds of assignments that match their own professional development plans, the committee could work with them to identify the appropriate cases.

As mentioned previously, associates must maintain responsibility for their own development, even if the pro bono committee makes every effort to provide them with the experiences they need. Rachel Strong affirmed, "Professional development is a 50/50 deal. The competency model will help associates along the path toward professional development, but it is still up to the individuals to be successful."

The Pro Bono Committee works closely with the Training and Professional Development Committee and the Performance Evaluation Committee to ensure the associates are getting the professional development experiences that they need to succeed. For example, if the Performance Evaluation Committee identifies a specific competency that an associate needs to achieve, the evaluator can refer the associate to the Pro Bono Committee for a case that will give him or her that experience. This process addresses the firm's dual goals of assisting indigent clients who need the firm's help and contributing to the growth and training of the associates.

Performance Evaluation Committee

Our Performance Evaluation Committee was looking for ways to improve the evaluation process and became a partner in the creation of core competencies and their connection to associate performance.

The committee wanted to implement an evaluation system that used a common language and could hold up to a standard measurement. Ed Han, chair of this committee summarized the goal as a way "to develop an evaluation process that gives associates specific guidance as to the skills and achievements they must demonstrate in order to advance professionally." The committee welcomed the competency model as a way to accomplish that.

Assignment Committee

Our firm's Assignment Committee monitors the assignments of each of the associates, particularly when the associates are new to the firm. With the implementation of the competency model, there has been even more focus on making assignments that not only meet the partner and client needs, but also enhance associates' skill sets.

The Assignment Committee looks for ways to best utilize associates skill sets. However, this is a subsidiary goal to the committee's true purpose. "There are other places in the system where associates can get the training they need," Chair James Kress explained. "When the committee makes an assignment, it first looks for associates who are appropriate for the case and who comply with requests of the partners. The committee rarely tries to force the partner to provide a particular assignment to an associate just for the sake of providing experience."

The competency model provides the committee with better information about associates and their capabilities. "When trying to make a match, we will have much richer anecdotal information about their skills and the information will be much easier to access," Kress said. "We're actually dealing with solid information rather than someone's preconceived notions about an associate's skills."

Kress looks forward to the day when there is a database record of associates' skills. "Right now, the Performance Evaluation Committee hears more about people than other people in the firm do. They get a great deal of feedback, both good and bad, on the associates' skill and experience levels. The competency model will help synthesize this information and will provide a richer file so that the assignment process will be based on objective data rather than anecdotal evidence."

Diversity Committee

Our Diversity Committee viewed the model as another tool to ensure that the development of women and minorities is handled fairly—in short, a method that develops the skills of all attorneys.

Partnership Committee

Associates want a clearly defined path toward partnership. Linking the competencies to that path is critical. Your partnership committee may already articulate the necessary criteria for partnership, and now it must help link each criterion to the relevant competencies in the model. Essentially, the partnership criteria won't change, but it will be expressed in a common language that can be used in training, feedback, and promotion considerations.

A New Path to Partner	
The competency model you develop must relate in concrete, well-articulated ways to your associates' ultimate goal: partnership in the firm. Solicit your firm's partnership committee to help align the expectations for partner to specific competencies in the model.	
LEVEL I PARTNER EXPECTATIONS	RELATED COMPETENCIES
Handling all aspects of complex regulatory matters and litigation, particularly trials and other in-court proceedings.	<ul><li>Mastery of Substantive and Procedural Law</li><li>Trial and Courtroom Skills</li><li>Written Advocacy</li><li>Oral Advocacy</li><li>Negotiation Skills</li></ul>
Billable and total hours that reflect a substantial commitment to the firm and its clients.	<ul><li>Growing the Business</li><li>Client Service and Communication</li></ul>
Working cooperatively with others; supervision or training of others in constructive ways; and similar contributions to the firm's well being.	<ul><li>Working Cooperatively and Effectively with Others</li><li>Project/Case Management</li></ul>
Meaningful involvement in and support for the internal and external initiatives, governance, policies, and practices of the firm.	<ul><li>Leadership</li><li>Internal Communication and Support</li></ul>
Significant contributions to bar associations, pro bono involvement, and other professional and community activities.	<ul><li>Developing Self</li><li>Drive for Excellence</li></ul>
Strict adherence to the high professional and ethical standards in all firms, client, and other work-related activities.	<ul><li>Drive for Excellence</li></ul>

The development of a viable competency model can seem like an arduous task—and it is. It takes planning, the involvement of people at every level of the firm, and communication. The time and commitment are worth the effort when the results show a successful strengthening of the learning culture of your organization, the improved service to clients, higher morale, and increased productivity.

A Shift in Culture

Corporate America has proved that using competency systems for employee evaluations can enhance a business's ability to create a high-performance culture—a corporate culture that values, expects, and teaches its employees to perform their jobs at the highest levels possible. Even if your firm is not reticent to innovate or take chances, you'll notice that as your business grows, your philosophy with regard to the training of your attorneys will need to change. Perhaps you, too, will find that your competency initiative should focus on training and creating a high-performance learning culture at the firm—a very positive benefit of developing and implementing a competency initiative.

Researcher and author Jim Collins describes the distinguishing factors between companies who "get by" and those who become industry leaders in his book, *Good to Great: Why Some Companies Make the Leap...And Others Don't*. "The good-to-great companies understand that doing what you are good at will only make you good; focusing solely on what you can potentially do better than any other organization is the only path to greatness."

Accordingly, part of your goal to establish a viable competency model should be to focus your attorneys on the competencies that will make them—and in turn the firm—best in class. Of course, there are many competencies that could be included in your program, but you must choose the vital few that address your specific foundational needs.

Another goal in shifting your firm's culture may be to create a stronger learning environment. Peter Senge, MIT professor and founding chairperson of the Society for Organizational Learning, said in *The Fifth Discipline*, "The organizations that will truly excel in the future will be the organizations that discover how to tap people's commitment and capacity to learn at all levels in an organization." Debra Snider, former general counsel of Heller Financial and author of *The Productive Culture Blueprint*, puts it another way: "The productive culture is one of inclusion, shared values, and opportunity. These elements are what make it possible for people to add unique value, defined in terms of the company's business objectives and strategies."

This statement is especially true for professional service firms that are only as good as the knowledge and expertise they have to offer to clients. Building the knowledge and skills of a professional service staff is equivalent to improving a product in a manufacturing company. Keeping those skills sharp and up-to-date requires a culture with learning and training at its core.

Consider how your firm would define a high-performance learning culture. Our firm defines a learning culture as "one in which people are continually learning, partners are teaching and coaching, and associates feel they are advancing their skill sets."

Bain and Company, a global international business consultant, justifies our definition. "Too often company culture is viewed as a 'given' and not as a strategic lever to adjust in line with strategy and changing competitive dynamics. 'High-performance' organizations recognize the power of culture to drive performance and know when it needs upgrading. Changing an organization's culture can play a critical role in lifting a company's performance trajectory." Bain points out that a successful culture matches a firm's strategic aspirations. "To be competitive, organizations must continuously strive to overcome poor performance and achieve higher productivity at all levels across all jobs."

Culture is important. It can be a predictor of an organization's performance and profitability. James Kotter and James Heskett, Harvard Business School professors, found that creating cultures that align the interests of clients, employees, and shareholders are more likely to be profitable and survive over time.

Competencies Linked to Supporting Systems

Training & Development
What are the development
requirements for our jobs?

Performance Management
How should employees be
evaluated and coached on the job?

Succession Planning
What are the succession
requirements for our
organization?

Competency Model

Career Decisions
How should qualified
employees be rewarded
and promoted?

Organizational Change
How should we communicate
our culture and our brand image?

Recruitment/Selection
How should qualified external
candidates be identified?

A successful competency model will link to all the systems that make your firm function—from training and development to recruiting and succession planning.

If your firm develops and utilizes a competency model—adapting it to your own long-term strategic vision and successfully incorporating it into your culture—you should be able to identify the skills and behaviors that define the profile of a successful attorney and enhance the firm culture. The individual or specific competencies you identify as desirable for your attorneys need to align with the firm's mission and provide a common language for associate development, as well as a focus for feedback, training, and coaching. The model should offer clear behavioral examples of performance expectations, as well as a roadmap for the professional development and advancement of individual attorneys. Your goal should be to enlist the entire firm (associates, partners, and practice groups) in the development and utilization of the model to identify the key competencies necessary for success, align the competencies with processes for developing talent, and make the competencies an integral part of firm culture. If successful in this complex mission, the performance level of all attorneys—and therefore the firm—will rise.

The Training Factor

Let's step back and look at what may prompt you to make a radical change in the learning culture of your firm. Young attorneys joining your firm as associates fresh out of law school rarely have much practical legal or business experience. And in this economic environment where corporate clients are trimming the number of firms they employ, the practice of law—the running of a law firm—is as much a business as a service, no doubt about it. Clients must be served to the best of the firm's ability, retained over the long term, and satisfied from year to year. Only the best talent can make this happen, both on the partner level and on the associate level. But, with associates' limited practical experience, this is difficult to achieve efficiently. Training programs are needed, but it is difficult to make them consistent and efficient.

There are a number of traditional approaches used by law firms to train their associates. Some firms provide in-house training programs run solely by partners. Other firms combine this in-house approach with some outside-the-firm training. There are firms who make finding training opportunities the sole responsibility of the associates.

Many firms have used the traditional apprentice model as one way to train their associates. Under this system, senior attorneys take on younger attorneys as apprentices and allow them to shadow the senior attorneys and watch them in court. The associates receive individual feedback and coaching and are able to learn at least some of the necessary lawyerly skills they need. But their training under this model is not systematically defined and organized, nor is it managed with an eye to the overarching needs of the firm.

Terre Rushton, Associate Director of In-House Programs at the National Institute of Trial Advocacy (NITA) in Louisville, Colorado, said, "The apprentice model is classic and works to a certain degree. It should not be discarded, because it is always a good experience for associates to watch good trial lawyers. But learning by doing is a better kind of learning. It's intellectual and visceral, the skills are portable, and the learner becomes responsible for his or her own success."

As firms grow, associate training often shifts away from the apprentice model for several reasons: time, the increasing number of associates to be trained, and clients who restrict the number of junior attorneys who are allowed to attend meetings or go to court. Associate training understandably becomes even more fragmented. Seen as an almost a secondary issue—training can be done when there's time, when there's a pressing need, or when someone else organizes it—this approach (or lack thereof) makes it difficult to ensure comprehensive or strategic training of any kind.

When analyzing associate training, you may ask two key questions:

- Are our associates acquiring all the skills they need to be successful?
- Is the firm teaching skill sets it needs to stay competitive in the future?

A competency model can provide you with a way for your firm to systematically identify, organize, and define critical associate skills. It will help you identify and hire the best candidates, provide a clear professional development path for all associates, and proactively make available the training that your associates need.

A competency model can serve your firm well on a number of fronts, but especially with regard to training. A well-structured competency model provides a systematic process to manage and develop associate talent. It can provide insights on how best to spend training and recruiting dollars. A clear competency model can enhance long-term business strategy by providing a means to evaluate the qualifications of recruits and provide consistent training for newly hired associates. If a system can be developed and then used consistently over several years, your firm will begin to see better trained, well rounded, seasoned partners.

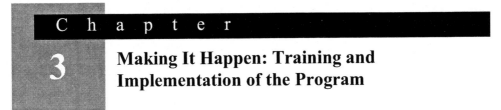

Chapter

3 Making It Happen: Training and Implementation of the Program

You've reached a critical point in the development of your competency model. You've convinced firm leadership that the model is necessary to the overall growth of the firm, and you have created your list of specific competencies. There are two more steps left to complete your initiative: creating the training component and implementing the model throughout the firm.

Creating the Training Component: The Case for Training

According to *The War for Talent*, professionals "want the company to help them develop their skills. This is particularly important today, when people realize that their only real security in the job market is the collection of skills they possess."

It's important to position your competency model as part of your value proposition to associates. When you hire an associate, there are probably several features that attracted him or her to your firm—potential work experiences, firm culture, and salary, to name a few. Your training program, if developed properly, will also be a selling point for new associates. Remember that even after they are hired, associates may continue to ask themselves if they have made the right decision in joining your firm. Is the value proposition of working at your firm greater than what they'd find at another? As associates start their professional lives and continue to evaluate their answers to this question, attrition rises and falls. You want to make sure that after all the time and money your firm has spent to recruit and hire candidates they remain at the firm and become contributing, productive members.

Answer these questions honestly:

- Why would a talented person want to work here?
- What does our firm offer that others don't?
- How can our firm develop associate talent to the fullest potential?
- If we promise specialized training, how will we follow through on that commitment?

Persuasive value propositions are usually customized to the needs of specific talent segments and typically include comprehensive training opportunities, as well as work assignments that are demanding, that stretch the individual, and that are interesting and worthwhile. Creating these opportunities for growth and development will involve many of your administrative committees or the equivalent. The committees involved with associate development need to be coordinated and aligned with your defined value proposition. Integrate their work into your competency model and maintain it throughout the associates' career cycles. Although all of your committees probably will play important roles in the development of your training curriculum, your training and professional development committee will most likely drive the process.

Training Trends in the Legal Environment

We asked several partners and managers what they thought was lacking in the way law students are trained. We wondered what law schools could be doing better in order to provide law firms with ready-to-work attorneys. The answer that came up most often was the perception that law students do not receive enough hands-on, practical experience in law school.

Martin Cunniff, the chair of our firm's Training and Professional Development Committee, said, "Law students have the potential to be ready to work when they graduate, but they are not ready right out of school. When it comes to litigation, the ability to read cases has little to do with fixing a dispute. The development of good skills (the soft skills), such as management [and] organization, is often more important than being able to evaluate the law."

Further, students do not learn management principles that are important to their work. Mary Craig Calkins noted that law students "are not trained in the business of law. Attorneys at all levels need to realize that in order to satisfy clients, associates need to approach their work as part of running the business—not just on the substantive issues of law but also in practical terms."

True, law schools provide soon-to-be associates with the intellectual knowledge of how the legal system works along with basic legal knowledge, but specific skills, such as how to depose a witness or how to build persuasive motions, are generally left to the employer.

If your firm focuses on litigation matters, you'll create a curriculum that allows associates to become proficient in those competencies. Outside organizations, such as NITA, are available to create customized programs targeting specific skills in a safe, risk-free environment.

Terre Rushton explained, "The atmosphere for good learning needs to be risk free. When it comes to teaching associates, they need to be reassured that it's OK to take risks."

Consultant organizations can offer associates a practice ground for building a case for the client, advocating for the client, and learning oral advocacy and trial skills.

Organizing Around Client Needs

As clients' own business needs change, some worry about having their cases used as training grounds for associates. If existing training is driven by the time and initiative of local partners, it may leave associates to rely solely on real cases to learn skills. The result may be an uneven and limited development of skills, because not every case will provide the experiences associates need to become well-rounded attorneys. For our firm, core competencies help alleviate some of those worries by identifying the competencies for success. The model offers attorneys a compass to ensure that training offered by the firm is both consistent and comprehensive.

Joanne Caruso, the managing partner of the Southern California office, said, "The competency model is important to clients for two reasons. First, it shows clients that the firm has a proactive training program that will systematically identify and provide the skills clients expect associates to have. Second, it shows clients that the training associates receive will be done on our time and at our expense. It is important for clients to know that the work they assign to our associates will be opportunities for our associates to apply what they already know instead of being opportunities for our associates to learn something new."

With a newly created model, the primary goal of the training and development committee can be simple—at least on the surface: to formulate a strategy to ensure that associates consistently develop their skills and continually progress in their careers. The underlying development is more arduous, of course, but your first priority is to build a training curriculum based on the competency model, and this committee should address several key issues with associates:

- Explaining how the competency model was developed;
- Demonstrating how the model links to the training curriculum;
- Defining the levels associates should be demonstrating within each competency;
- Explaining mastery expectations with regard to competencies that may not apply to an associate's chosen practice area;
- Making the model accessible to both regional and international offices;
- Helping associates link their development to performance evaluations; and

> ▪ Articulating the firm's expectations for how many training hours associates should commit to.

Learning Methods

Since people learn differently, we wanted our program to include several different ways for associates to learn the skills we want them to master. We followed these approaches:

> ▪ Identified competency development opportunities in associate orientation presentations, pro bono work, classroom training, and e-learning.
> ▪ Linked the performance evaluation process to professional development. We created a way for associates to be empowered to develop their skills through their own initiative by providing evaluation feedback and appropriate development resources.
> ▪ Created a standard curriculum for each associate level and provided opportunities for associates to customize their learning based on their own needs.
> ▪ Designed programs using adult learning theory. Adults build skills through experience—doing, practicing, and getting feedback on their performance. They gain knowledge through reading and watching. A well-rounded training should include a variety of learning methods.

Classroom Training

Classroom training is the traditional training vehicle for building knowledge and skills. Knowledge can be gained through lectures, reading, hearing principles, and watching speakers or panels. To build actual skill, however, people must be able to practice and receive constructive feedback as they try the new skill.

When developing classroom experiences for our associates, we wanted to make sure it included ways for them to put their new knowledge to use through practical, real-world experiences. We took advantage of outside, national program initiatives to include learning-by-doing experiences, which encourage actual skill development (as opposed to head knowledge). This learning can be put to use when associates take on pro bono cases, and then again when they handle actual matters for paying clients.

E-learning

E-learning—also known as web-based learning, computer-based training, or distance learning—can include a variety of training options. Law firms are quickly following Corporate America in the movement to incorporate e-learning into their training plans because it is efficient and convenient. E-learning allows attorneys to control the speed of the lessons. They can move quickly through the content they understand and slow down to take in new and complex material.

E-learning also is beneficial for just-in-time training needs, such as when a CLE requirement is due or when an online refresher is needed for a particular case or matter. Thanks to the wonders of intranet technology, most e-learning courses can be made accessible 24 hours a day from almost anywhere.

E-learning is often the best vehicle to ensure the consistent dissemination of information. For example, we have used it to develop a firm orientation presentation. It includes video messages from the managing partner about the vision and values of the firm, as well as information about the practice. This type of learning vehicle is less expensive than other formats. *Training Magazine* found that mixing classroom training with e-learning experiences can save organizations 50 to 70 percent of training costs. However, e-learning is limited in skill development and lends itself more to information transfer.

Developmental Components of the Competency Model

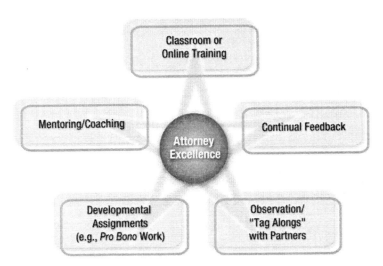

Make sure you provide as many types of learning experiences as you can for your associates. According to adult learning theory, people learn different things in different environments, and no two people learn the same way. Use these various methods as you create development opportunities for your associates.

Howrey Academies: Building Foundational Skills

In building our training program, we articulated learning objectives for each associate level. We determined which learning objectives were focused on providing knowledge and which ones required skill building, as this impacts the instructional design of the courses. We wanted programs that included both lectures and hands-on experiences. We asked attorneys to share their actual courtroom or trial experiences (including the do's and don'ts of preparation and presentation), which allow the associates to absorb the information in a very usable context.

Long-time NITA faculty member Sanford M. Brook stresses the importance of these presentations. "The presentations are not just lectures. When a NITA faculty member shares fundamental skills, he or she presents how the activity should be done, juxtaposed with how it should not be done, and then the skills are demonstrated in a real-world context. The faculty member involves the associates by inviting questions and answers and providing opportunities for drills and demonstrations."

We created associate academies to teach foundational skills to three levels of associates: junior, mid-level, and advanced. These are taught by both internal and external subject matter experts. For example, we tap the knowledge of our partners and the expertise of NITA to create and present our three-day, off-site seminars.

Brook said that the structure of this type of session should be carefully planned: presentations should be made right before the associates are given the opportunity to practice their new skills, and the new skills should be reinforced by written materials the associates can take away for future reference.

Overall, the academies aim to:

- Build and reinforce superior advocacy skills as specifically identified in the competency model;
- Provide firm-wide training to support the firm goal of becoming a single integrated firm that shares a common skill base;
- Set the firm apart from the competition by providing a systematic curriculum that attracts and retains top talent;
- Teach both the hard skills (actual processes such as taking and defending depositions) and the soft skills (such as client service and leading teams) needed by all attorneys; and
- Reflect the firm's commitment to overall associate development.

We integrate the hard and soft skills at each associate level:

- The Junior Associate Academy (for second- and third-year associates)
  - o Fact Investigation and Oral Advocacy: Depositions and Motions
  - o Drive for Excellence: Meeting Partner Expectations
  - o Working with Others: Contributing to Effective Teams

- Mid-Level Associate Academy (for third- and fourth-year associates)
  - o Trial Skills
  - o Advanced Fact Investigation
  - o Project Management and Communication

- Senior Associate Academy (for fifth-year and beyond associates)
  - o Advanced Oral Advocacy
  - o Growing the Business: Client Service
  - o Leadership and Professional Responsibility

In the academies, associates receive individual feedback on their strengths and developmental needs. While this ultimately helps them formulate their own professional development plans during the performance evaluation process, their work during the academies is not included in their evaluations, which helps create the safe, risk-free learning environment. In fact, mistakes almost are encouraged because they provide such good learning experiences—and don't cost a client or the firm additional funding.

Fiona Chaney, a second-year associate on our Associate Affairs Committee described the information she received at the first academy she attended as practical and useful. Since training hours are not billable hours, she said the program was presented as a way for the attending associates to check another skill off their competency list, which provided additional motivation to attend.

Diedra Grant, a third-year associate said the Mid-Level Academy, which focused on courtroom skills, gave her the individual, detailed attention and instruction she needed to address areas she considered weak.

We found the learning-by-doing approach beneficial to both associates and partners. First, the partners serving as training faculty use the opportunity to refresh their own skills as they prepare for their teaching experiences. They also learn a great deal from NITA instructions on how to give feedback. For example, our partners are taught that they need to identify the specific behavior that did not go well and model how it could have been better demonstrated. This approach to giving feedback focuses less on the person and more on the actual competency or behavior.

We found a second benefit of having firm partners participate as academy faculty: it sent a message that learning is valued by the firm. Associates see that partners are taking time out of their schedules to teach and coach.

Recruiting partners to serve as faculty can be challenging. Our Training and Professional Development Committee chair was instrumental in volunteering his time as faculty and asking his peers to also volunteer. We found this partner-to-partner invitation very effective in eliciting participation.

Associate Training

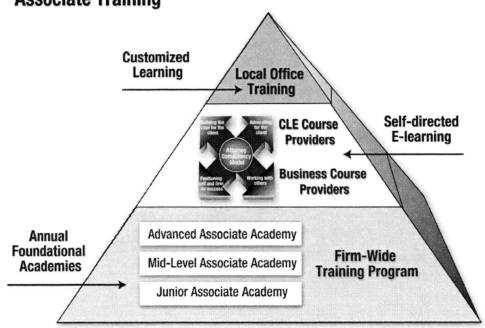

Howrey's training experiences create a pyramid of learning opportunities that build from one to another, each enhancing the next.

Local Training

Although firm-wide academies that bring associates together from all offices are valuable, local training is equally important to the development of associates. Issues that are specific to local jurisdictions can be dealt with directly, and associates and partners are given the opportunity to work together in ways that facilitate coaching and mentoring.

At Howrey, there is a local training partner for each office. These partners form committees that determine regional training needs and provide in-house education on subjects that are of interest to their associates. This structure achieves two goals: it promotes a learning culture by encouraging partner/associate interaction at the local level, and it leverages local partners' subject matter expertise. While local partners lead this effort, they also empower associates to suggest ideas or to share information with their colleagues at these sessions. As an aside, although broadcasting these programs via videoconferencing seems like a good idea, we have found it difficult for the offices on the receiving end to engage with the speakers and now rarely use it as a training vehicle.

Senior Associate Training Day

At our firm, associates who are in or beyond their fifth year are eligible to be senior associates. Promotion to this level occurs before the associates are considered for partner. We have found it very helpful to provide a day of special training for this group. The newly-named senior associates come to a particular office to celebrate their promotions and to learn some business development and client relationship skills. The day's program is comprised of external speakers who lecture on how to grow the business and provide quality client service as well as information on how associates at this pre-partner level should market and develop themselves. A panel of experienced firm partners then share advice and lessons learned with the group as well.

Virtual University for E-Learning

Our firm also wanted to offer learning experiences online. Therefore, we created a virtual university called Howrey U. The initiative enables associates to manage their training individually, proactively, and on their own time. The format enables firm attorneys and staff to learn without having to leave their offices. Our goal is to make Howrey U a single, comprehensive source of professional development resources for our attorneys and staff.

Howrey U is designed to look like a virtual campus with "buildings" dedicated to different functions:

Howrey U Campus

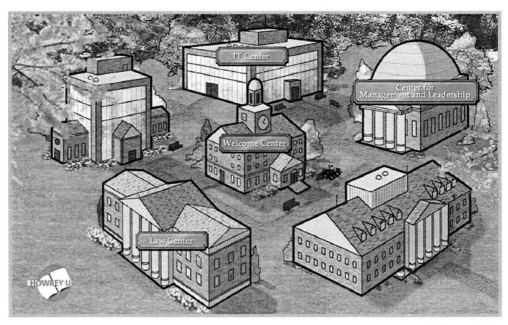

© Howrey LLP

The Howrey online virtual campus—Howrey U—has been developed with an eye to being attractive and inviting. Each building shown on the opening page of the intranet site links to a part of the overall training program. The Law Center houses the complete list of competencies, along with the rationale for how the model was developed and how it will be used and links to other areas of the site. This building is also where the competency czars live. The Center for Management and Leadership building houses online management and continuing legal education (CLE) courses and a CLE tracking program. The IT building houses all computer-related resources.

The Welcome Center provides background information a newcomer to the site needs and includes:

- A "tour" of the campus;
- Frequently asked questions;
- Contact information for staff in various offices who can provide additional information about navigating the resource and related professional development; and
- A feedback form.

Intranet Site Design

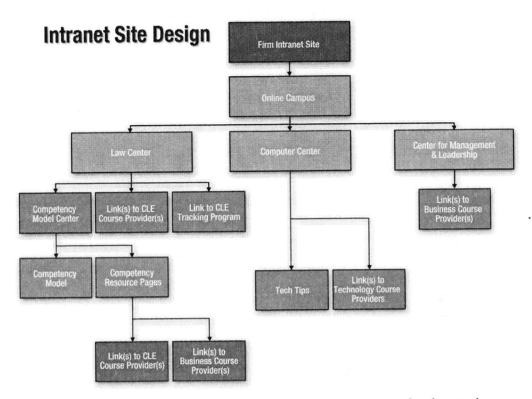

Like the model itself, Howrey U's intranet site design is clearly organized and is simple to navigate. Links are provided in all the appropriate places so that resources are accessible and easy to find.

There are many ways to organize your online learning. For example, you may organize it by function, as opposed to skill, which we have done in our design model.

The Law Center is the crux of Howrey U. It houses:

- All the attorney training resources;
- A complete list of the competencies;
- The rationale for developing the competency model;
- Contact information for the training partners;
- An explanation of how the competency model is used in performance evaluations;
- Links to a continuing legal education (CLE) tracking program; and
- Links to vendor web-based libraries of materials that can be used to fulfill MCLE requirements and further professional development. Specifically, these materials will cover the skills in the Mastering Substantive Areas of the Law competency. Providers' libraries typically include webcasts, video, and audio programs.

The Center for Management and Leadership houses programming specifics regarding soft skills—such as management, leadership, communication, strategy, and decision-making—flagged in our competency model (e.g., Project Management, Keeping Teams on Target, Leading a Team, and Capitalizing on Change). The online business-related programs—most of them outside the legal arena—feature a breadth of management and leadership content and the integration of curriculum, resources, and activities. They feature interactive practice exercises with the reality of on-the-job and workplace scenarios, audio, and resources and tools to meet everyday business needs. The IT Center provides technical computer-related information for attorneys—everything from how to use Microsoft Excel to tips for managing technology. The IT Center includes:

- Quick tips for using all the software programs the firm employs
- Access to e-learning courses, resources, and certifications on software applications including Microsoft Office courses at a variety of levels—from introductory to expert

Evaluation and Measurement

To assess return on investment of our training efforts, we send out a comprehensive evaluation form after each academy and have a scorecard to track local training efforts (see the Toolkit for both).

The qualitative comments help us understand our associate mindset and what motivates them. One associate said of our training, "I came with a relatively closed mind to the whole thing, but I did a complete 180. Not only did I learn a lot, but I had a lot of fun learning it. I took from the week a sense of what 'it' is all about. I became re-energized to do my job and do it well. Even though document review is still going to be boring at times, at least I have first-hand knowledge of what the end result is, and that will help during the tedious times."

The Personal Touch

Online programs are useful learning resources for associates and junior partners because they allow a self-serve approach to learning. But nothing compares to the insider perspective—we asked several of our partners to serve as "competency czars" for various subjects that correlate to specific competencies. We selected these czars from within the firm as subject matter experts to provide resources, ideas, and tips on development for each competency. These partners aren't mentors as much as they will become online sources of helpful information for the benefit of all associates.

Our business development competency czar, Martha Gooding, created ideas, tips, and what she calls "war stories" for associates to use as online resources, in addition to compiling books and articles of interest to associates who are developing their business development competency (see the Toolkit for the full text).

She explained, "We don't expect young associates to bring in business—they're not ready yet. But they can lay the groundwork by networking, participating in professional and community activities, writing or assisting in the writing of articles, and the like. Then, as their practices mature, they will have a solid foundation for generating new business. Client service is a broad activity that can reap benefits in business development. Every piece of work a lawyer does is business development."

Associate Development Committee Integration

Howrey's Training and Professional Development Committee ensures that associate development occurs not only in the training classroom and through e-learning, but also on the job and through pro bono assignments, depending on how a specific competency is best learned. The Training and Professional Development Committee coordinates with each of the other committees to identify ways associates can build their competencies in a variety of arenas outside of formal training. Similarly, it can build strong bridges between associate development and evaluation feedback.

Pro Bono Committee

From the beginning, our pro bono committee has been an essential part of the development of our training program. Pro bono cases give associates real-life experiences and provide hands-on opportunities to use their skills. Since most cases go to trial and are concluded within a year, these cases are excellent training grounds for new associates.

The goal of our pro bono committee is to consider an associate's competency needs when matching him or her with an appropriate case. The committee selects and tailors the types of cases that are recommended for each class year to address the related competencies. Another goal of the committee is to educate the partnership about the value that pro bono work can add to the competency model so that this work becomes an integral part of the model. Additionally, it is important to the committee to maintain junior partner involvement in order to accept cases that provide second-chair roles for senior associates.

In developing pro bono-related training opportunities, your committee may identify several issues that need to be addressed with associates. For example:

- Defining the kinds of cases the firm considers to be pro bono cases;
- Determining how billable hours will be handled when associates work on pro bono cases;
- Defining the number of pro bono hours an associate may bill;
- Identifying the number of pro bono hours the firm expects associates to bill;
- Articulating how pro bono assignments can be used to build competencies;
- Helping associates identify pro bono opportunities; and
- Providing a solution to the problem that occurs if a pro bono case does not provide the necessary competencies an associate needs to master.

The challenge is to clearly identify the competencies that can be achieved within every case.

As the competency model begins to roll out at your firm, consider asking your committee to identify cases that will help associates complete their professional development goals and match those cases to the appropriate associates. For instance, many first-year associates need to improve their writing skills. Therefore, the committee should select cases where writing briefs is an essential part of the assignment. "Law students are gung ho and ready to take on the world when they graduate, but because many cases settle before trial, they don't get the stand-up experience they hoped for," Howrey Pro Bono Partner Rachel Strong pointed out. "Pro bono cases allow associates to gain stand-up experience right away. This gives them confidence and allows associates to use that law school energy immediately.

"If a case settles, the associate may be frustrated, but they've still had a real experience," she said. "They have had client contact and possibly written and argued a motion. The associates and the Pro Bono Committee know that the next case the associates work on will be another opportunity to garner the experience they need."

To make sure the committee is providing the right kinds of experiences for associates, each participating attorney fills out an evaluation form (see the Toolkit for the example Pro Bono Closure Form). This form asks the attorneys to describe in detail the different professional development experiences gained from the case. The feedback provides the committee with the continuing information it needs to continue selecting the appropriate cases for the firm's associates.

Diversity Committee

As we rolled out the competency model, our Diversity Committee goals were to:

- Ensure that minorities and women have opportunities through case assignments to develop and succeed at the competencies; and
- Address any systematic biases that may prevent objective evaluation of the performance of minorities and women in the competency areas.

We wanted to ensure that our Performance Evaluation Committee had an awareness of systematic biases that might occur in the evaluation process and had a training workshop to that end. To ensure that minority associates have access to the right kinds of experiences as they move along their professional development path, your diversity committee may work with your professional development and training committees to develop post-case surveys to glean feedback from the associates.

Although the training plans that emerged from our competency system have been the fulcrum of our rollout, we wanted to ensure that the competency model aligns with the work of all of our associate development committees—especially the Performance Evaluation Committee. We plan to keep a fluid and flexible approach to the competency integration to allow for changes as the business needs of the firm evolve. Over time, we hope to see improvement in attorney performance at all levels.

Implementing the Model: Beyond Training

With your competency initiative developed and articulated and your training curriculum formulated, you're ready to implement and roll out the whole program and make it part of your associate talent-management processes and your firm's culture. Start by identifying the committees that will be impacted by the model, as well as the owners of particular processes—for example, the firm leaders who own performance evaluation or pro bono assignments, if there are no specific committees for these functions. As the champion of the process, your role will be to clearly express your expectations for each committee. Ask each committee to put together an action plan for incorporating the competency model into their work and coach them to complete the plans.

Typically, the committees that will be impacted by your competency model will include:

- Training and professional development;
- Pro bono;
- Diversity;
- Performance evaluation;
- Assignment;
- Recruiting; and
- Partnership.

Committees Impacted by the Competency Model

All of your administrative committees will be impacted by your competency model. Make sure each one has an opportunity to contribute to the development of your model as well as to its implementation.

As we implemented the competency model and presented it to the firm, our communications—memos, brochures, or in-person presentations—included information about how the model was developed in a participatory style that reflected cross-firm voices. Additionally, these communications stressed that management and the partnership support the program.

Performance Evaluation Committee

One of the primary goals of your competency model may be to provide associates with clear, objective feedback on their performance. We learned that the evaluation process can be frustrating for associates, particularly if they feel they were not getting enough feedback and that the expectations of the firm for their professional development were not clearly defined or expressed. Our partners saw the need for a change in the system as well, and expressed a desire that evaluations be done with a common language and treat everyone fairly, from office to office and practice to practice.

Fiona Chaney, a member of the Associate Development Committee described the system as fair. "It is just one model; we don't have different models for everyone at every level. It gives us guidance from day one and is a valid tool for managing our careers. Associates want to grow without competition and the competency model provides the guidelines for this growth. It is very helpful for modeling one's career, carrying out the path."

Using a competency model will likely change your method for evaluating associates. We designed new forms to define each competency at different levels of mastery (see the Toolkit for a sample evaluation form) so that the reviewing partners can measure the performance of the associates with concrete examples of our competency levels.

Associates prepare self-evaluations in the same way. The performance evaluation committee can review partner evaluations along with the self-evaluations from the associates. The system provides a way for the committee to go back to the reviewing partners to ask more questions, if it feels something was left out of the evaluation, or if a partner doesn't understand a particular competency.

Chances are that this method will offer associates more clarity regarding how they are evaluated than they have ever seen. When the committee reviews the evaluation with the associate, each partner will have provided performance feedback that is thoughtful, concise, and to the point. After receiving this feedback, the associate creates an individual development plan and identifies two or three areas where improvement is needed to work on through the year. This lays the groundwork for the objectives that associates must accomplish to develop best professionally.

Performance Management Process

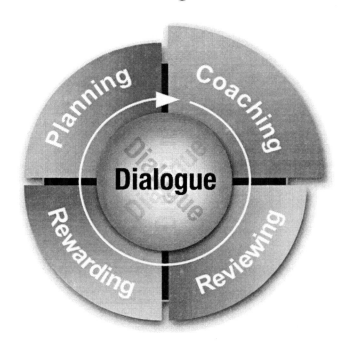

Managing your firm's talent is a continuous process that is based in dialogue. Once you have planned how your process will work, it is critical to provide coaching, opportunities for both formal and informal performance reviews, and, of course, rewards that are appropriate to the level of development achieved.

Once core competencies are implemented, associates may grapple with whether they must master every competency at every level regardless of their practice group. A foundational competency model may need to be flexible enough to complement all practice groups. We created foundational competencies that are not too specific or apply to only one area to address this issue.

Training the Evaluators

Since we created a new performance evaluation system, it was important to educate partners about its nuances. Under the new system, the partners have to think differently about the way they evaluate the associates who work for them. The partners who may have previously been advocates for their associates now have to be more objective. The partners who rated associates highly must now provide examples of associates' work. This new system of evaluation takes more time, and partners have to be convinced that it will be time well spent.

Howrey partners were advised on standard evaluation biases and how to prevent rating errors and biases from creeping into their evaluations. These errors can include:

- *General Bias Errors:* When raters are either too severe or too lenient in their ratings of all associates and do not take into account the individual associate's actual job performance.
- *The Halo/Horn Effect:* When raters let an assessment of the associate on one task influence their overall rating of the associate.
- *Logical Rating Errors:* When raters give the associate a high score on one task because it is related to another task that the associate performed well.
- *Contrast and Similarity Errors:* When raters judge associates based on how they perceive themselves as either similar to or different from the associate.
- *Central Tendency Errors:* When raters are reluctant to make extreme judgments about associates, avoiding the extremes on the rating scale, which results in a narrow range of scores.
- *Proximity Errors:* When raters have a tendency to be influenced by how they rated surrounding competencies (e.g., if the associate was rated high for competency No. 2, then the rater may tend to carry over the favorable response as it applies to the associate's performance on competency No. 3, even if it is inappropriate).
- *Rating Inflation:* When a partner's ratings tend to increase over time without justification. The partner should make sure the ratings are based on results, not the feeling that ratings should increase.

Assignment Committee

Your assignment committee may benefit from the competency model and the data that will be collected through the performance evaluation system. Historically, our assignment committee has focused on filling partner requests for associates who can perform specific tasks on individual cases or matters. Requesting partners often have preconceived notions about which associates are "good" or "average" performers based solely on anecdotal evidence. By collecting data on associates' performance within each competency, the assignment process will become more objective and more informed. It will provide your assignment committee with more data to advocate for a capable associate who may not be well-known or who may be mistakenly perceived as an average performer because of one task in one situation that may not have gone well.

Recruiting Committee

Another area of the competency integration is recruiting. All firms vie for talent, and a competency model can be used to rate skills and behaviors of prospective hires. Hiring associates and laterals who show mastery of the competencies you think are important can result in less attrition, better-qualified candidates, and more immediate enhancement of the firm's bottom line.

Similar to the performance evaluation committee, our recruiting committee reviewed its hiring process to accommodate the new competencies. The existing interview process needed to be redesigned to become more structured and incorporate behavioral event interviews (see the Toolkit for additional information on how to revise this type of interview for recruiting purposes).

Ideally, the competency model should be flexible enough to use for hiring both new associates (new graduates or judicial clerks) and laterals. Interviews with new associates might focus on the more general competencies, given candidates' limited experience. Lateral hiring might benefit from a more structured process because those candidates have more work and life experience to discuss during the interview process. Over time, this approach to hiring may raise the level of overall performance of the firm's individual attorneys.

Rollout of Changes

Rolling out a competency model can create high levels of fear among associates, especially when they discover that it will impact their performance evaluations. To alleviate some of these fears, we followed these change-management principles:

- Explain the rationale behind the new model and the benefits of using the model in all the committee areas.
- Create a consistent message for all offices.
- Test the message with a sample of associates.
- Identify partner spokespeople to deliver the message.
- Enlist associate representatives to be champions and provide feedback on reactions.
- Create a Frequently Asked Questions sheet (see the Toolkit for an example) for associates to refer to.
- Provide ample opportunities for feedback, clarification, and discussion.

We also found the following checklist helpful:

Rollout Checklist

✓ Identify the firm leader who will be the sponsor of the competency model and support its integration into associate development.

✓ Identify the committees that own the success of the competency integration.

✓ Identify the partner and associate champions in each office.

✓ Identify the people who will develop your communication plan.

✓ Develop a system to ensure feedback from all stakeholders as the initiative progresses.

During rollout, we created a slideshow with embedded video clips from the committee chairs and involved development staff explaining the genesis of the competency model, the benefits to associates' careers, how the model was developed, and how it will be integrated into pro bono work, performance evaluations, and training.

We identified one to two partners in each office who served on the Training and Performance Evaluation Committees to deliver the presentation, distribute the competency model and the FAQ sheets, and answer questions. We set a three-week time frame for the offices to complete their rollout to ensure that associates received the messages directly from their local partners and didn't rely on rumors from their peers. Before the rollout of the model, we called associates representatives in each office to enlist their help in underscoring the benefits of the model and help keep a positive outlook on the rollout.

Obviously, with any change, it's helpful to solicit feedback from everyone. Our partners and the Associate Affairs Committee representatives' comments, concerns, and criticism helped us hone our presentations and keep our message clear and consistent.

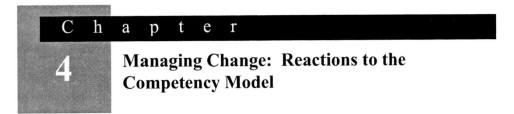

Chapter

4   Managing Change: Reactions to the Competency Model

We've talked about the importance of involving every part of your firm in the development, implementation, and integration of your competency model. Since associates are the ones who will be first and foremost affected by a competency model, we also found it important to monitor their reactions.

And you can expect mixed reaction, no matter how hard you've worked to communicate the value of your model. We found it important to focus on two issues: effectively managing change and knowing your audience.

Effectively Managing Change

People don't like change. This is a stark statement, especially in a world where change is inevitable: the economy can strengthen or weaken in a heartbeat, the seeming whim of one general counsel can drastically alter—for better or worse—a law firm's profit margin, a new performance evaluation system can completely rearrange the process by which associates develop to become law firm partners. Change can be frightening, but you can successfully manage people's reaction to it by understanding the psychological and emotional stages they go through when confronted with what they perceive as upheaval.

Individual Transition and Personal Reaction

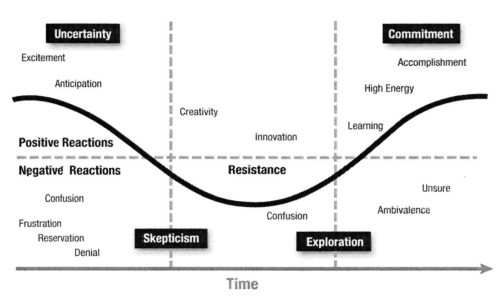

The stages of change are predictable, even though they are deeply felt personal emotions. Understanding that your associates (and quite possibly some of your partners) are going to be uncertain and skeptical at the beginning will help you help them to reach the point of committing to the change wholeheartedly. You need to communicate often and consistently, and then you need to be patient as this natural process runs its course.

William Bridges, author of *Managing Transitions,* explains that there are three stages that people go through when dealing with change:

1. Endings;
2. The neutral zone; and
3. Beginnings.

Each stage is accompanied by specific emotions. To manage any change successfully—especially one as sweeping as implementing a competency model—you need to acknowledge people's emotions and help them through each stage by providing communication, support, and explanations of the rationale or structural components of the change. For example, in the ending stage, people will experience feelings of loss, which may be accompanied by emotions of anger, anxiety, sadness, or disorientation. Your role will be to acknowledge those feelings and help them understand that loss is part of the change process. Not everyone will feel these emotions or experience them intensely, but in any group of people, you can expect to encounter some of them. Continue to communicate why you're making changes related to your competency model, and reassure your people by defining what is different about the new program and what will remain the same. Explain why you are moving to a one-firm competency model approach for training, professional development, and performance evaluations, especially to those associates and partners who might have liked the flexibility of having different expectations in each office without the constraints of a shared model.

In the neutral zone, people adjust to the pending change, but they haven't fully experienced it yet. In this zone, signals are often mixed and there are ambiguities that can cause people to polarize either for or against the change. This period also is a creative time, as it opens up new possibilities for those involved. Emotions can include excitement, anxiety, tension, and frustration. It's important to allow people to have a voice at this stage—both to air their concerns and share their ideas. Some associates may be concerned that the model won't fit their professional development or that the new training won't be a valuable use of their time. Similarly, partners may be concerned about "losing" key associates for training time, and they may be anxious about having to learn how to evaluate associates using a more disciplined and rigorous measurement system. Address these concerns and emotions by keeping your message consistent and on point.

Finally, the beginning stage marks the acceptance of the new way of doing things—your model is finally launched and implemented for training and performance evaluations. But there still may be fear and anxiety as people try out the new systems. You probably will experience that as your associates and partners will go through the three emotional stages as your competency model rolls out and you begin to enforce the new programs. Through it all, make sure that you have established a good system for taking in—and responding to—all feedback. Allow everyone to share their emotions and ideas about how to improve things.

According to Bridges, there will always be resistance to change. Another blunt statement, to be sure, but we found it helpful because it allowed us to deal with resistance constructively. Resistance is a main reason that change efforts fail, but there are other reasons, as well.

Be mindful of these change-blocking elements as you develop and roll out your competency model. Systematically addressing each one helped us smooth our transition to the new program.

- *Limitations of existing systems:* Address all the systems and processes that will be affected by your competency model.
- *Lack of executive commitment:* Make sure leadership is fully supportive.
- *Lack of executive champion:* Identify the experts and champions needed for the model to be successful.

- *Unrealistic expectations:* Articulate the firm's expectations in a way that everyone understands.
- *Lack of cross-functional team:* Enlist the support of both internal and external experts who can help deliver your message and teach the needed skills.
- *Inadequate team and user skills:* Provide training and coaching for everyone who will use the new system.
- *Staff and users not involved:* Inform associates, as well as staff, that a new system is being developed.
- *Project charter too narrow:* Define charter of initiative appropriately.

Your new competency initiative may well be perceived as a radical change in your firm's culture. Reaction to this change can be emotional, and many will take it personally at least to some degree. Communicating to everyone involved with the model can be helpful in managing change and enabling its acceptance.

Questions we found helpful as we reviewed the communication materials included:

- Is our message consistent?
- Is it clear?
- Has it been vetted by everyone who will have to present it and by representatives of those who will ultimately receive it?

Enabling change is an ongoing process and as we made our first presentations, we found ways to refine the communication methods for easier, quicker acceptance without changing the content of the message.

A helpful formula was:

Need for Change
+
Clear, Shared Vision
+
Management Commitment and Behavior
+
People Involvement
+
Supporting Structure and Process
+
<u>Performance Measures</u>
Lasting Change

We included the need for change in the business case for building a competency model, along with the shared vision and commitment of management. Getting our partners to commit to serving as training faculty, coaching them so they were up-to-speed with the new evaluation and recruiting processes, and putting our leadership champions out in front of the model reflected management commitment. Involving associates, partners, and committees in the development of the model provided people involvement. The committees provided processes and structure, and obtained feedback.

We distributed communication to everyone in the firm in as many forms as possible. Most of the communications addressed the following questions:

- What are we doing and why?
- How does the change relate to our business strategy?
- Why will we be more competitive with this new system? Does the change make sense?
- What processes and structures will be affected?
- Is management really committed?
- What is the change plan? Is it doable?
- Is it being done fairly?

After communicating, we allowed for a waiting process, which gave each individual time to accept the change and start functioning within the new model. Here are the questions they answered as they made the final, personal resolution to move ahead:

- What are we doing and why?
- How will the change work, and how does it affect me?
- How do I know it will be successful?
- You know what? If we modified it here, it might work.
- *OK, let's run with it.*

We have reiterated the need for regular communication during every phase of the development of your model. The firm's leadership is important as well. We asked our leader-champions to visibly participate and provide the right kind of role modeling. Each time they spoke about the competencies was another opportunity to "sell" the model, whether to each other or to affected associates. If, for some reason, the partners don't understand some element of the program, your message may become skewed and unfocused, and associates will be unsure that they can trust the touted benefits of the model.

Consider a marathon run as an example: Like transition, marathons are "run" at different paces by different people. In a marathon, the runners at the front of the pack are off immediately once the gun goes off. But the people in the back might not have even heard the gun and may only notice the start through word of mouth from other runners. Sooner or later the people in the back begin to move their legs and take small strides; meanwhile, the front-runners are well into the race. Sometime later, as the runners at the back just begin to hit their stride, the first runners are crossing the finish line.

As employees progress along the change continuum, some may loop back to an earlier phase. The route to successful change is not always the same, nor is it always forward or "in synch" with everyone else.

Another natural reaction to a change in systems is a drop-off in performance at the beginning. As people deal with the overall effect of the change on themselves, their energies may go to places other than their work. As they become comfortable with the change and see positive benefits, their work productivity will come back and they will continue to improve.

Knowing Your Audience: Associate Support and Resistance

While many of your associates may support a new system and appreciate the clear direction it gives them, there may be resistance that might come from associates who don't see the obvious benefits right away. Change is difficult to manage under the best of circumstances, but for your youngest employees (either in age or seniority), change can be downright frightening.

Let's face it: life as a first-year associate at a big law firm can be bewildering. Law school was difficult, but it was structured and students' environments (classes, professors, and assignments) changed regularly as they progressed from semester to semester, year to year. The recruiting process, while challenging, was also structured. Associates-to-be may have had plenty of support from their law school's career development offices and feel good to be courted by your firm, but the reality will hit after they start in the office.

Suddenly, these first-year associates are on their own in a new way. Those who have never held full-time jobs prior to joining the firm realize that the day in, day out sameness of working lacks the luster and glamour they anticipated. This is certainly a concern of associates, but partners are also affected by associates' lack of experience.

One of our partners notes that the disconnect is hard to overcome. "There should be a prerequisite that students work for two years before going to law school," he advocated. "They need to get into a routine: working a 40-hour week, understanding how to own a problem, dealing with superiors and clients. Too often very bright associates are not able to get their bearings when they come to work at a firm."

Amid the adjustment angst, the professional development department expects associates to create career goals and professional development plans, attend training sessions that don't seem to fit with what they're currently working on, and recognize that the evaluation process has been revised. It's quite a bit to cope with—the seven-to-eight-year path toward partner seems bumpier than expected. It also reinforces how important it is for you to manage the changes, since they will set the tone for the ultimate acceptance of the model.

Associate Reaction to the Competency Model

We found it helpful to keep updating our associates on the development of our competency model—involving associates from every class, from the building of the competencies themselves to the final implementation of the initiative. By adjusting the competency model and implementation based on associate input, we noticed that, for the most part, their reactions were positive, enthusiastic, and optimistic. At the same time, however, there also has been resistance and skepticism. We've dealt with theses mixed reactions by first understanding where the associates were on the stages-of-change continuum. We addressed their concerns by making sure we had incorporated all the elements of the Lasting Change Formula. Finally, we engaged the more enthusiastic associates in the change management process by having them communicate and reassure the resistant associates.

Reaction to Rollout of the Model

The subgroup of our Associate Affairs Committee assisted with the integration of the model into the overall culture of the firm. This group collected general feedback and used that input as a tool to integrate the model.

With just two cases completed, first-year associate Ashley Bass is enthusiastic about the model. "The competency model will help us see ahead on a yearly progression," she believes. "It will show where we should be among our peers. It will help us search out opportunities if we are not getting the experiences we want."

Senior associates didn't necessarily share the first-year associates' enthusiasm.

Bronagh Hollywood, the firm's Human Resources Legal Analyst, understands those associates' anxiety. She explained, "Associates are concerned about getting the opportunity to demonstrate specific competencies on cases."

Jan Brown, Manager of Attorney Recruiting, added, "Not all practice areas require all competencies to the same degree. For example, patent prosecution does not emphasize trial and courtroom skills as much as global litigation does."

As mentioned previously, your pro bono committee may be able to assist by offering them volunteer assignments focused on the areas in which they crave exposure.

Some of our associates found the new firm professional development model no more than a public relations or marketing ploy. We addressed this by keeping communication lines open, even after the model was set. We accepted the positive feedback and took seriously the negative comments we received. We offered success stories to demonstrate the positive benefits of working within the model that included reference to the competencies and included the competencies in training announcements.

Others held fast to their belief that their evaluations would depend solely on the partners they work for and the luck of the draw in terms of the assignments they receive. We shared the revised evaluation forms, which showcase how ties to competencies will be encompassed.

And yet others remain quietly positive as they wait to see how the new system actually affects their lives as attorneys. We continue to solicit opinions and suggestions from this group.

One associate articulated the model as Bass had—that it will "provide benchmarks and goals to help measure my progress and to give me something concrete for which to strive."

Her hesitation with a full embrace, however, was proof that it is actually the formula for success. "I just need to see it play out for the classes ahead of me to be assured that it works as intended and that it will be actually enforced—that if I hit all the requirements I will make partner, rather than the situation where I'd be told that I've hit the requirements, but because of limited numbers of partner openings I don't make it."

Reaction to Training

As with most initiatives, our competency-based training program garners both praise and doubt.

We found it helpful to solicit lawyer insights via anonymous feedback forms after every training to keep our finger on the pulse of their opinions.

There was negative commentary, even resentment for taking away from the time associates have to complete billable assignments during the first trainings, particularly from more senior associates. Consistent reinforcement of how the skills impact their life at the firm helps them overcome these reactions.

Reaction to Evaluation Process

Initially associates' biggest concerns lie in how the performance evaluation system affects them. COO Koenen said, "Associates may be nervous; they won't know how to perceive the model and how it will tie to evaluation and advancement decisions."

First-year associates were not the only ones to feel concern. Our upper-level, more senior associates were concerned about how their lives will change under the new system.

Training and Professional Development Committee Partner Will Um said, "They are concerned about whether they'll move ahead if they haven't been trained under the competency model."

During the initial rollout, the competency model generated a negative as opposed to a positive impression at our firm—specifically, our lawyers feared that it was nothing more than an outline of ways for associates to fail, particularly at the senior level. Even if viewed in this light, creating a sense of urgency for your associates to take a close look at their career development before they reach the threshold of becoming partners is actually a good idea.

We tried to calm associates and still get them to examine their careers by using the following communications:

- Create a fact sheet that explains how the model is linked to evaluations.
- Send e-mails to address the concerns of associates in your offices overseas. Of course, there are extreme differences in the practice of law in, for example, Europe, when compared to the United States. This issue is the impetus for building flexibility into the model so that these associates can be evaluated on the essence of the competencies rather than the exact letter of the model.
- Make presentations in each office to all local training committees. These frank sessions ensure that partners understand why associates are anxious to be involved in cases that will help them master specific skills and balance the work among them. These meetings helped us provide some associates with opportunities they might not have received, had they not spoken up.

The way firms "use the competency model in terms of evaluations will be very important. It will affect credibility if people perceive that the competencies are holding them back in some way," Um noted.

"One way to balance this is to formalize the items on the skills list and make sure everyone understands that this should not be merely a checklist of items where the goal is to get the most check marks. We still need to impress on the associates that the job needs to be done well; we need good reviews from clients; and associates need good reviews from partners."

Over time, we hope associates will appreciate having their evaluations tied to a competency model. It will improve morale because the tie will put remarks on a common plane.

Communicate and Revise

It is important to continue to communicate the goals of the competency initiative, even when you think it is safely implemented. Communication is a two-way street, and feedback is crucial. Take the comments of concerned associates, as well as those of any disgruntled partners, into account and address these concerns patiently and thoroughly—more than once, if you have to. If your associates think your competencies are "engraved tablets" that will be used against them, show the associates how they will benefit from the learning experiences you are offering. Enlist your firm's leadership and make them cheerleaders and approachable champions of the model. When an associate succeeds, let everyone know.

As Competency Czar Martha Gooding said, a competency model "should be motivational. Mastering the competencies should feel doable, but the firm is not doing the work for the associates. It should make development of the competencies seem less daunting to the associates." At the same time, Gooding noted that "the firm should provide training, but the associates should not wait to have opportunities thrust upon them." She tells associates, "You should be proactive: find partners to work with who will enhance your skill set. Your career doesn't just happen to you. You need to invest in yourself; get coaching if you need it."

COO Koenen said, "We will judge the success of the model when we see associates reaching higher levels of competence faster, when we see them understanding the business better, and when we see them developing into better leaders."

The competencies help ensure that clients are satisfied. Koenen believes that clients will judge a new firm program positively when they see the firm running more like a business.

When our firm identifies a problem, we try to address it quickly and openly. This helps everyone believe that the model is flexible and that it will grow and change as the firm evolves.

Above all, we remind people that the model was developed as a tool to make the firm better, more profitable, and better staffed. We found that keeping everyone's eyes on the goals of a competency model was important for the model to succeed.

Toolkit

Competency Model Toolkit

Tool 1: Communications

Tool 2: Competency Model Development and Implementation Tools

Tool

1   Communications

The following memos illustrate the various ways you can communicate to the many factions in your firm.

Memo 1

TO: Executive Committee
            Business Operations Group
            Office Managing Partners
RE: Attorney Competency Study

The Training Committee is attempting to identify key competencies by associate level to help us design a training curriculum. We have contracted with an outside consultant to develop an initial competency model for attorneys.

The initial study will focus on key technical and soft skills that should be foundational for every associate and will not be practice area specific. The consulting group is a leader in understanding and identifying how individuals impact and increase organizational success, and is an expert in developing competency models of this type.

In the coming weeks, selected partners and associates from all offices will be asked to participate in panel discussions to identify tasks, core competencies, and other top performance indicators for associates and junior partners. The results will become the foundation of our associate training program. This model will also be shared with the Performance Evaluation Committee in supporting its efforts to provide a common basis for feedback, evaluation, and coaching.

Memo 2

TO: Local Office Leadership

RE: Attorney Competency Study

As you may be aware, the firm has recently contracted with an outside consulting group to develop a competency model for associates and junior partners. This consulting group is a leader in understanding how people impact organizational success and an expert in developing competency models of this type.

In the coming weeks, selected partners and associates from all offices will be ask to participate in panel discussions in order to identify tasks and competencies that associates and junior partners need to be considered high performers at the firm. This information will be used to create a competency model that will include the attributes and behaviors that will become the foundation of our associate training program. This model will also be used by the Performance Evaluation Committee to provide a common basis for feedback, evaluating, and coaching, and to provide clear behavioral examples of expectations.

Memo 3

TO: All Partners

RE: Attorney Competency Study

In the coming weeks, the outside consulting group recently hired by the firm will be conducting panel discussions with selected partners and associates in order to develop a competency model for associates and junior partners. These consultants are leaders in understanding how people impact organizational success and an expert in developing competency models of this type.

During this phase of the project, the consultants will be gathering information to identify the competencies associates and junior partners need to be high performers at the firm. This information will be used to create a competency model that will include the attributes and behaviors that will then become the foundation of our associate training program. This model will also be used by the Performance Evaluation Committee to provide a common basis for feedback, evaluating, and coaching, and to provide clear behavioral examples of expectations.

If you are asked to participate, I hope that you will be able to find time in your schedule to attend and share your thoughts on this important topic.

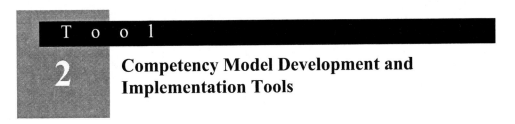

Competency Model Development and Implementation Tools

There are several tools that you can use to help develop and implement your competency model. The pieces included in this section can be modified for use in your particular environment or they can be used as is.

Behavioral Event Interview

What follows is an example of a behavioral event interview. Notice that the purpose of this type of interview is to determine not only the experience level of the person being interviewed, but also how the person handled specific situations. The questions are designed to elicit conversation. This interview approach will help you discover more about your interviewees and will help prevent them from telling you what they think you want to hear.

Note that this type of interview works very well as a recruiting tool as well. Start the interview with statement below. (Note: At the beginning of each question, ask the interviewee to start by describing the event in one or two sentences so you will have an idea of what he or she is going to be talking about).

"The purpose of this interview is to learn about you and some of the key experiences of your legal career thus far. I will ask you to talk in detail about some significant work-related events, one at a time. These events should have occurred recently enough for you to talk about them in detail—preferably within the past year or so.

"I know that teamwork is often an important aspect of case work; however, for the purpose of this interview we want to find out what your individual involvement was in each particular event or situation. As you describe these events, tell me what actually happened, focusing on your involvement in the situation. Specifically:

- What led up to the situation?
- Who was involved?
- What did you do and say at the time?
- What did you think and feel at the time?
- What was the final outcome of the event or situation?"

Follow-up questions can be used or not, based on how you feel the interview is going and what the person says.

The following questions, based specifically on competencies found in the model, will elicit where the interviewee fits in terms of mastery of skills.

Building the Case for the Client: Legal Research and Analysis

- "Tell me about a time when you performed the research requested and were able to locate the appropriate 'on-point' authority or information to solve the problem presented."

Factual Development and Investigation

- "Describe a situation in which you had to collect information by asking many questions of several people."

Creative Problem Solving

- "Give me an example of a time when you had to keep from speaking or making a decision because you did not have enough information."
- "Give me an example of a time when you had to reach a decision quickly."
- "Give me an example of a time when you used your fact-finding skills to solve a problem."

Advocating for the Client: Oral Advocacy

- "Tell me about a time when–either one-on-one or within a group setting—you had to express ideas or opinions so others would understand or be persuaded. This could be in a trial or pre-trial situation, or even in meetings with witnesses or team members."
- "What steps did you take in influencing others?"
- "How did you determine the tactics you would take?"
- "What challenges or obstacles did you face?"
- "What was the outcome of your efforts?"

Negotiation Skills

- "Describe a time when you handled negotiations with other parties or agencies (these do not need to be formal negotiations)."
- "What role did you play in the negotiations?"
- "What challenges or obstacles did you face in reaching an agreement?"

- "Can you tell me a little bit about the interactions you had with the opposing side or person you were negotiating with?"
- "What were the results (or outcome) of the negotiations for you? For your client?"

Trial and Courtroom Skills

- "Tell me about a time when you played a critical role in the proceedings or outcome of a trial."
- "What role did you play in the pre-trial preparation?" (Then follow up with probes about what the interviewee did specifically.)
- "Did you have to personally address any objections? If so, tell me a little about how you went about doing that?"
- "Who else was on your team?"
- "Were there any challenges in working with or managing team members?"
- "Did you have to change focus or strategy at any point? If so, what occurred and what was your role in doing so?"
- "What was the outcome of the trial/event?"
- "What was the outcome of this event for you personally?"

Working with Others: Project/Case Management

- "Tell me about a job or project where you had to gather information from many different sources and then create something with the information."
- "Tell me about some project management methodologies you have found to be most effective."
- "Give me an example of a time when management had to change a plan or approach to which you were committed. How did you feel and how did you explain the change to your team?"
- "Tell me about a time when you had to juggle multiple projects."

Leadership

- "Tell me about a time when you formally or informally led a group of people on a task, project, or case."
- "What was the task, project, or case?"
- "How did you come to lead the group?"
- "What was your role in terms of working with or leading others?"
- "What specific actions did you take in leading the group toward your goal?"

- "Did you have to convince others to approach things differently or your way? If so, how did you go about doing that?"
- "Did this entail helping someone else develop his or her skills, knowledge, or competencies? If so, how did you go about doing that?"
- "What were the results (or outcome) for you? For the group? For the client?"

Working Cooperatively and Effectively with Others

- "Describe a time when you proactively and willingly helped team members—taking up the slack when needed—without seeking individual/personal credit."
- "Tell me about a time when you publicly credited more junior associates who have performed well."
- "Describe a time when you resolved team conflicts."

Internal Communication and Support

- "Tell me about a situation when you had to speak assertively in order to get a point across that was important to you."
- "Describe a time when you provided complete and thorough support to other lawyers, allowing them to concentrate on other matters."
- "What experience have you had in making oral presentations?"
- "How do you rate your skills in this area?"

Positioning Self and Firm for Success: Client Service and Communication

- "Tell me about a time when you did your best to resolve a client concern and the individual still was not satisfied. What did you do next?"
- "Describe a time in which you provided extraordinarily good service, above the call of duty to a customer or client."
- "Give me an example of a time when you went out of your way to meet an agreement."

Drive for Excellence

- "Give me an example of a time when you went above and beyond the call of duty."
- "Describe a situation when you were able to have a positive influence on the actions of others."
- "Describe some projects or ideas (not necessarily your own) that were implemented, or carried out successfully primarily because of your efforts."

- "Tell me about a time when you worked to accomplish a challenging goal."
- "What was the goal?"
- "How was the goal initially set?"
- "What did you do to work toward the goal? What steps did you take?"
- "What obstacles did you encounter while working toward the goal?"
- "What critical issues or problems did you face?"
- "What was the outcome that you achieved?"

Growing the Business

- "Describe how you would establish a network of contacts in the business and legal communities."
- "Tell me about a time when you took action to expand business with existing clients and developed new business."

Developing Self

- "Tell me about a time that you had to learn a new skill in order to do your job."
- "After participating in a learning activity, how do you bring that knowledge back to the workplace?"
- "Tell me about a time that you had to seek new ideas and approaches to allow you to complete a project."
- Tell me about a time when you had to actively solicit formal and informal feedback on your own performance."

Attorney Local Office Training Scorecard

This form can be used to solicit feedback from associates after training sessions. It can be used in each local office (middle columns) and can be easily adapted to fit your firm's needs. Note the reference to "Survey Monkey." Survey Monkey is an online service that creates professional surveys that can be completed in real time (www.surveymonkey.com).

Criteria	1	2	3	Description
Attorney Satisfaction Ratings				
1. Course Ratings				Ratings after each in-house seminar (look at average for each of 5 questions and overall rating)
2. Year-End Training Satisfaction Survey				Survey Monkey assessment sent to all associates (and partners—with slightly different questions) to determine firm-wide training health, as well as that of local office. Sample questions: ✓ Extent to which training met your needs ✓ Area in which you would like more training Completed once a year
Local Office Training Offerings				
3. Number of Local Office Training Programs				Number of programs offered to all attorneys (does not need to be live program)
4. Number of Local Office New-Associate Orientation Programs				Local office orientation—number of programs offered (does not need to be live program)
Participation Rates				
5. Online Management Course Usage Rate				Number of attorneys who took online courses/number of attorneys in office (%)
6. Online CLE Usage Rate				Number of attorneys who took CLE courses/number of attorneys in office (%)
7. Local Office Training Attendance Rate				Average number of attorneys who attend programs/number of attorneys in office (%)
8. Individual Development Plan (IDP) Participation Rate				Number of associates who submit IDPs/number of associates in office (%)

Outcome Measures			
9. Associate Competency Ratings			Associate end-of-year ratings on competencies (aggregates by office, by competency on new Performance Management Process (PMP) form)
10. Individual Development Plan Results			Number of associates who fully meet their IDP goals at the end of the year/number of associates with IDPs (%)

Frequently Asked Questions

Create fact sheets that cover the common questions you face when you develop your competency model. We found it to be a good idea to have these sheets ready to pass out at each meeting where we made presentations. Both partners and associates found them useful.

Competency Model Fact Sheet

Professional Development

Why was the competency model developed?

The competency model was developed to identify and understand those competencies present in outstanding attorneys today and those needed to achieve outstanding individual and firm performance in the future. There were several driving forces behind the decision to develop this model: first, to provide associates with a clear roadmap for their development; second, to have one firm language for feedback, training, and coaching; and third, to provide clear behavioral examples of performance expectations and integrate training with performance evaluations.

How does the competency model link to attorney curriculum?

The attorney curriculum will be based on the competency model. Some competencies are more conducive to learning in a classroom setting and others can be learned on the job, through pro bono or self-guided learning (e.g., PLI or Harvard ManageMentor). There will be foundational academies, which will be based on the competency model. In addition, competency czars will serve as subject matter experts to provide online learning resources. The area of substantive mastery of the law will be covered primarily through your practice areas and local office training partners.

Am I responsible for mastering all competencies regardless of practice area?

The competency model was developed for all associates; however, we recognize that not all competencies are equally relevant but will have greater emphasis depending on level and practice area. This will be taken into consideration in how it is applied to associate development.

European law is different from U.S. law. How does the competency model apply to us?

The European partners who were interviewed during the competency model development thought there were more commonalities than differences. Rather than have a separate European competency model, they preferred to have a one-firm model and then adjust as needed through local office training.

How can my performance evaluation guide my development?

Following your performance evaluation, you will complete an individual development plan that focuses on three to four development priorities for the coming year. It will be your responsibility to complete the development goals, and they will be reviewed in the subsequent evaluation process. The associate academies are foundational courses and completion of these will be a factor in becoming a senior associate.

What are the expectations for annual hours of training?

The firm is committed to ensuring that we have superior skills underlying our client work and to helping associates meet their highest career potential. To this end, we expect all attorneys to meet all MCLE state requirements and to invest a minimum of 40 hours per year in training.

How was the competency model developed?

The firm hired an outside consulting group to guide the competency model development. They held meetings or conducted interviews in all offices. Overall, 90 attorneys representing all levels (associates and partners) and practice areas defined the 16 core competencies and the corresponding definitions.

Performance Evaluation

To what extent will I have to master all competencies to be promoted?

The degree of mastery required for each competency will depend on the nature of your practice group and the level of your seniority. The Evaluations Subcommittee will take into account differences in the competencies required for a particular associate for purposes of promotion.

What if the assignments I receive do not allow me to develop all of the competencies?

The Evaluations Subcommittee will work closely with the training, assignment, and pro bono committees to provide opportunities to develop the competencies that are required for each associate.

Will the competencies be exclusive method for evaluations?

No. The Evaluations Subcommittee will continue to solicit evaluations from partners with whom the associate has worked during the relevant evaluation period. Forms filled out by associates and partners will be modified to incorporate the competencies. The subcommittee will use evaluations, along with other available information (eligible hours, firm contribution, etc.), to make recommendations to the Executive Committee regarding an associate's overall performance.

Diversity

What role does the Diversity Committee have in the implementation of the competency model?

While all associates at the firm are expected to succeed on their own abilities and merit, the firm is taking steps to ensure that no one group of associates has any advantage with respect to succeeding at the competencies. The Diversity Committee will work with the training, performance evaluation, assignment, and pro bono committees to ensure that women and minority associates are provided the opportunities necessary to develop the competencies. The Diversity Committee also periodically will monitor the work experiences of minority and women attorneys as an additional check that minority and women associates are being provided the necessary opportunities.

Does the fact that the Diversity Committee has a role in this process mean that the firm has a problem in this area?

No. The firm is taking proactive steps to ensure that problems do not develop. Many corporations, including our own clients, have programs, policies, and training in place that address diversity issues. Taking these proactive steps in the area of diversity does not mean there is a problem, but is a best practice for all businesses.

How can women and minority associates best utilize the Diversity Committee in this process?

Women and minority associates, like all associates, should work with the training, assignment, and pro bono committees to seek opportunities to develop the competencies. They also should feel free to discuss any issues or concerns that arise with respect to their development and work experiences with members of the Diversity Committee.

Recruiting

How can the competency model support recruiting efforts?

The competency model describes competencies that the firm seeks in its professionals. This will enable us to focus hiring interviews and evaluations on acquiring data from the applicant that speaks directly to the existence of those competencies in the applicant.

Will interview guides and selection processes focus on particular hiring competencies?

Yes, when we are looking for specific competencies for specific class levels and specific practice groups. We will also look for competencies that are needed across the board, regardless of class or practice group.

How will this differ for new hires vs. laterals?

The competencies for new hires (new graduates or judicial clerks) will be more general given their limited experience. Lateral hiring will benefit more from a structured process, because laterals have more work and life experience to discuss during the interview process.

Who will be hired through the new interview process? Will the new hiring process be applied to all levels?

The new interview process will apply to all associate and of counsel new hires. It will not apply to partners.

Will there be training to accompany the rollout?

Yes, because interviewers will need to understand the need for a more structured process, and they will be trained to ask questions based on an understanding of the competencies, attitudes, and behaviors of successful lawyers at the firm.

Will the structured interview process be implemented firm wide?

Yes, the initial rollout will begin in the firm's headquarters and other offices will follow.

Why is a new process necessary?

A structured interview process will provide more and different information (interviewers in non-structured interviews tend to ask the same or similar questions). This will make the interview process more efficient for the firm and more interesting for the candidates, leading to better hiring decisions on both sides.

Pro Bono

What kinds of cases does the firm consider to be pro bono?

Consistent with ABA Model Rule 6.1 and the Pro Bono Challenge Statement of Principles, the firm defines *pro bono representation* as activities of the firm undertaken normally without expectation of fee and not in the course of ordinary commercial practice, and consisting of:

- Delivery of legal services to persons of limited means or to charitable, religious, civic, community, governmental, and educational organizations in matters that are designed primarily to address the needs of persons of limited means;
- The provision of legal assistance to individuals, groups, or organizations seeking to secure or protect civil rights, civil liberties, or public rights; and
- The provision of legal assistance to charitable, religious, civic, community governmental, and educational organizations in matters in furtherance of their organizational purposes, where the payment of

standard legal fees would significantly deplete the organization's economic resources or would be otherwise inappropriate.

If I work on a pro bono case, will I get billable credit?

Hours spent on firm-approved pro bono matters are treated for all purposes like hours spent on billable matters (i.e., they are fully counted in determining associate compensation and bonuses). To obtain approval for a matter, an attorney must fill out a Request for Approval Form, which must be approved by the pro bono counsel and the pro bono partner in charge of that particular office. In deciding whether to authorize the pro bono representation, the partner will consider:

- Whether the case fulfills the objectives of the pro bono program;
- The staffing needs of the case;
- The expertise required for the representation;
- The public policy issues involved in the representation;
- The firm resources that will be needed for the representation;
- The merits of the case and the likelihood of success;
- The significance and potential impact of the case; and
- The current pro bono workload of the firm.

If a matter will require more than 100 hours of attorney time, the attorney requesting approval must also submit a preliminary budget to the Pro Bono Committee. Once a matter has been approved for pro bono representation, the firm will handle it like a matter for a paying client, with established budgets and review.

Is there a limit to the number of pro bono hours I can bill?

There is no limit to the number of hours that an attorney can bill to a firm-approved pro bono matter. Once that matter is complete, an attorney must obtain approval before working on any other pro bono matter.

Is there a target number of pro bono hours that the firm wants all associates to bill?

The Law Firm Pro Bono Challenge encourages attorneys to spend up to five percent of their time on pro bono matters. The firm challenges each attorney to spend at least five percent of their time on pro bono matters.

If I do community service, do I get billable credit?

Although the firm encourages attorneys to get involved in their communities, the firm only gives billable credit for pro bono cases that involve legal work as described above.

How can pro bono assignments be used to build competencies?

The Pro Bono Committee has chosen pro bono cases for each class year that we believe will build on the core competencies that are appropriate for that class year. We have compiled these cases into a chart that attorneys can use when choosing pro bono cases.

How can associates find out what pro bono opportunities are available?

Each office has a pro bono partner who is in charge of pro bono activities for that office. Attorneys who want to work on pro bono cases may talk to those partners about what opportunities are available. Additionally, each office has chosen public interest organizations that refer cases to the firm. A list of these organizations is found on the pro bono intranet site; an attorney may contact those organizations directly to find out what cases are available. Finally, an attorney can work with the pro bono counsel to find a case that fits both the attorney's interest and professional development needs.

What if the case doesn't end up providing the competencies we were hoping to work on?

While we cannot guarantee a particular result or experience on a pro bono case, we make every attempt to assess new cases to determine what types of professional development experiences they will deliver. To help in that effort, when a pro bono case ends, we ask the attorneys who worked on the case to complete the Pro Bono Closure Form. This form asks the attorney to describe in detail the different professional development experiences gained from the case. The form is used to assist the Pro Bono Committee in choosing future pro bono cases. If a case does not meet an attorney's expectations regarding competencies, the pro bono counsel will work with that individual attorney to find another pro bono case that might better meet those goals.

Partnership Committee

How does the competency model relate to being a Level 1 partner?

The competencies reinforce all the criteria that have traditionally been considered for becoming a Level 1 partner. Review the Partnership Committee criteria for more details.

Should all Level 1 partners exhibit mastery of the competencies?

Ideally yes; however, being an effective Level 1 partner may look slightly different from person to person depending on practice area, client demands, and the firm's overall firm strategy in the marketplace.

Training Academies Fact Sheet

What are the Training Academies?

They are a series of intensive training seminars that target associates of different levels at the firm.

What are the benefits to the firm?

There are four major benefits:

- They build and reinforce superior advocacy skills identified in the attorney competency model.
- They provide firm-wide training to support the goal of a single integrated firm with a common skill base.
- They set the firm apart from the competition by having a more systematic curriculum that attracts and retains top talent.
- They reflect the firm's commitment to associate development.

How will associates benefit by attending the Training Academies?

There are five major benefits:

- To develop competencies that will help associates be successful at the firm.
- To learn by doing.
- To receive individual feedback on strengths and development needs, and to assist with development planning.
- To network and build relationships across offices.
- To earn 15 to 20 hours of CLE credit.

When do the Training Academies roll out?

There are three different dates based on associate level:

- Junior Academy—October 2004
  Audience: rising second- and third-year associates
- Mid-Level Academy—Spring 2005
  Audience: third- and fourth-year associates
- Senior Academy—Spring 2005
  Audience: fifth-year and beyond associates

What is the sample curriculum for each Training Academy?

There are a number of critical skills that will be taught at each Training Academy:

Junior Academy:

- Fact Investigation and Oral Advocacy: Depositions and Motions
- Drive for Excellence: Meeting Partner Expectations
- Developing Self
- Working with Others: Contributing to Effective Teams

Mid-Level Academy

- Trial Skills
- Advanced Fact Investigation
- Project Management and Communication

Senior Academy

- Advanced Oral Advocacy
- Growing the Business/Client Service
- Leadership and Professional Responsibility

What is the expected attendance for associates for the Training Academies?

First priority will be given to the defined audience for each Training Academy. Others can register on a space-available basis. Associates are expected to attend all Training Academies before being promoted to senior associate (adjust this accordingly depending on your associate level).

Are training hours considered in associate evaluations?

Yes.

Is billable credit available for travel or attendance?

No. These Training Academies are considered a part of an associate's professional development and individual responsibility. Successful completion will be shared with assignment partners and the performance evaluation committee.

How do I register?

Register online through a link that will be sent in advance of each Training Academy. Remember to plan ahead to manage any client conflicts with our supervising partner.

Who do I contact if I have more questions?

Contact one of the members on the firm-wide training committee with any questions about Training Academy curriculum. Contact the Professional Development Department with any questions regarding logistics or registration.

Training Academy Evaluations

Use this form as a method for soliciting anonymous feedback from training participants. Each area of the curriculum is rated on a scale of one to five (a rating of five is the highest rating).

Please rate the faculty members you worked with.

(1 = Not Effective; 3 = Average; 5 = Very Effective)

Faculty	Not Effective		Average		Very Effective	N/A	Response Average
Name							
Name							
Name							
Name							

Please indicate the effectiveness of each demonstration/lecture on a scale of 1 to 5.

Date of Presentation:

Presentation	Not Effective		Average		Very Effective	N/A	Response Average
Welcome							
New Realities in E-Discovery							
NITA Introduction to the Program							
Fact Investigation: The Client Interview							
Communicating Effectively and Collaborating Successfully							
In your opinion, should the demonstration/lecture occur before or after the related exercise?			Total Response				
Before							
After							
Were the witnesses were well prepared?			Total Response				
Yes							
No							
Did the witnesses provide a realistic experience?			Total Response				
Yes							
No							

My personal expectations were met (please rate on a scale from 1 to 5).

Strongly Disagree		Neutral		Strongly Disagree	Response Average

Please indicate the statement that reflects your experience most accurately.
My knowledge about:

	Has Not Improved	Has Improved Somewhat	Has Greatly Improved
Overall Interview Strategy			
Case Analysis and Discovery Planning			
Witness Preparation			
Taking a Deposition			
Defending a Deposition			
Information Gathering			
Obtaining Admissions			
Theory Testing			
Motions to Compel Discovery			

Please indicate the statement that reflects your experience most accurately.
My ability to effectively:

	Has Not Improved	Has Improved Somewhat	Has Greatly Improved
Plan an Overall Interview Strategy			
Analyze the Case			
Prepare Witnesses			
Take a Deposition			
Defend a Deposition			
Gather Information			
Obtain Admissions			
Test Theories			
Argue Motions to Compel Discovery			

What aspects of the Training Academy were particularly effective?

❑ Practicing the skills
❑ Meeting in smaller groups to discuss objectives
❑ Requiring us to learn on our feet
❑ The deposition sessions
❑ Being able to practice the skills and receive feedback

What aspects of the Training Academy were not effective?

❑ The motions practice sessions
❑ The depositions defense portion
❑ Introductions before each objective
❑ The planning sessions for the motion to compel
❑ Client interviewing, defending witnesses
❑ Practice interview session

Please rate the following on a scale from 1 to 5:

	Strongly Disagree		Neutral		Strongly Agree	Response Average
This program contained significant current practical or intellectual content.						
The written materials contributed to the learning experience.						
The objectives stated in advance were satisfied						
Overall, this academy was a valuable learning experience.						
I would recommend holding this academy again.						

Please rate the following on a scale from 1 to 5:

	Very Poor		Average		Very Good	Response Average
Information/books and materials received before the academy						
The opportunity to network with peers from other offices						
Administration during the academy						
Hotel facilities						
Academy website						

Performance Evaluation Form

The following form is an example of the competency-based performance evaluation form. Evaluating partners are asked to give examples of how the associate performed specific tasks, which allows for a deeper evaluation than simply checking items off the list.

Competency Model—Assessment

Reviewee:	Position:
Reviewer:	Practice Group:
Evaluation Committee Member:	Eval. Period:

Hours that the reviewer worked on the matter(s) listed below. Reviewee billed at least 200 billable or 50 pro bono hours on the same matter(s):

Client Matter #	Client Name	Matter Name	Hours

Click here to see detail on shared matters. Please note: you only need to evaluate those competencies that the associate has demonstrated *(link to form)*.

(All fields above populated by evaluation system)

Describe the extent of your contact with the associate:
❑ Daily or almost daily contact
❑ Regular contact on continuing projects
❑ Occasional contact on several projects
❑ Infrequent contact on one or a few isolated projects
❑ Insufficient contact to evaluate

Please only provide an assessment on the competencies you have witnessed the individual perform. Note, some competencies may not be relevant based on this individuals current role, practice area and/or office location.

BUILDING THE CASE FOR THE CLIENT	**Proficiency Level**
LEGAL RESEARCH AND ANALYSIS	❑
FACTUAL DEVELOPMENT AND INVESTIGATION	❑
MASTERY OF SUBSTANTIVE AND PROCEDURAL LAW	❑
CREATIVE PROBLEM SOLVING	❑

ADVOCATING FOR THE CLIENT	
WRITTEN ADVOCACY	❑
ORAL ADVOCACY	❑
NEGOTIATION SKILLS	❑
TRIAL AND COURTROOM SKILLS	❑

WORKING WITH OTHERS

PROJECT/CASE MANAGEMENT ❏
LEADERSHIP ❏
WORKING COOPERATIVELY AND EFFECTIVELY WITH OTHERS ❏
INTERNAL COMMUNICATION AND SUPPORT ❏

POSITIONING SELF AND FIRM FOR SUCCESS

CLIENT SERVICE AND COMMUNICATION ❏
DRIVE FOR EXCELLENCE ❏
GROWING THE BUSINESS ❏
DEVELOPING SELF ❏

Legal Research and Analysis entails the ability to conduct legal research using appropriate journals, texts, documents, etc., and to analyze a legal problem.

1. **PERFORMS ACCURATE RESEARCH:**

   - Performs the research requested and is able to locate the appropriate "on-point" authority or information to solve the problem presented
   - Is familiar with and comfortable using basic legal research tools, including books and computerized research tools.
   - Updates and checks validity of authority and extends authority and information to find additional materials.
   - Performs analyses that are clear and legally supportable.
   - Uses appropriate level of effort for the task (i.e., performs the appropriate amount of research based on partner and case needs).

2. **TAKES INITIATIVE TO PERFORM COMPREHENSIVE RESEARCH:**

   - When appropriate, aggressively looks for and locates the most helpful authority, even when this entails going beyond the original assignment.
   - Uses research to redefine or narrow the research requested and locates useful authority or information, even if not directly on point.

   - Analogizes to other types of legal problems to find helpful authority and information.
   - Performs all types of legal and factual research using tools including statutory, legislative, regulatory, international, and obscure resources as necessary.

- Performs research that is thorough, creative and reflects in-depth analysis.
- Performing legal research proficiently—especially with computerized research tools—in a cost-effective manner.

3. RESEARCH STRATEGIST:

- Approaches legal problems on many different levels; can locate useful authority or information even on difficult issues, and performs analyses that result in novel or creative solutions.
- Evaluates research results and identifies additional research needs that may not be readily apparent.

4. DEFICIENT

- Does not demonstrate basic competency

5. NON-APPLICABLE

- Have not had opportunity to witness competency and/or competency does not apply to practice or position.

Associate:
Evaluating Partner:
Evaluation Committee Member:

You selected level _____.

Please provide specific examples and explanations to support the level you selected. If you do not provide support, the Evaluation Committee may have difficulty in utilizing your review.

Associate Self-Evaluation Form

This form is similar to the Performance Evaluation Form and is filled out by the reviewee prior to the performance evaluation process. It gives a great deal of detail about the associate's work during the evaluation period, which serves to assist the reviewer prepare his or her own evaluation.

2005 Pre-Evaluation Report: John Smith

Reviewee:	Position:
Reviewer:	Practice Group:
Evaluation Committee Member:	Eval. Period:

(All fields above populated by evaluation system)

1. Client Matter Task List: Matters on which this reviewee has billed at least 200 billable or 50 pro bono hours. Click on each client matter to provide additional detail.

Client Matter #   Client Name   Matter Name   Hours
(Client name and matter will be a link to task list)

2. Feedback to Committee
Please provide any additional information that you feel should be considered by the Evaluation Committee.
Click here to open the form. (*Link to feedback form*)

3. Attorney Competency Model
Please complete the Associate Self-Assessment (*shown immediately below*).
Click here to open the form. (*Link to competency model form*)

III. Competency Model—Self Assessment

Please assess yourself on competencies that are applicable to your position. Some competencies may not be relevant based on current role, practice area, and/or office location.

BUILDING THE CASE FOR THE CLIENT	**Proficiency Level**
LEGAL RESEARCH AND ANALYSIS	❏
FACTUAL DEVELOPMENT AND INVESTIGATION	❏
MASTERY OF SUBSTANTIVE AND PROCEDURAL LAW	❏
CREATIVE PROBLEM SOLVING	❏

ADVOCATING FOR THE CLIENT

     WRITTEN ADVOCACY   ❑
     ORAL ADVOCACY   ❑
     NEGOTIATION SKILLS   ❑
     TRIAL AND COURTROOM SKILLS   ❑

WORKING WITH OTHERS

     PROJECT/CASE MANAGEMENT   ❑
     LEADERSHIP   ❑
     WORKING COOPERATIVELY AND EFFECTIVELY WITH OTHERS   ❑
     INTERNAL COMMUNICATION AND SUPPORT   ❑

POSITIONING SELF AND FIRM FOR SUCCESS

     CLIENT SERVICE AND COMMUNICATION   ❑
     DRIVE FOR EXCELLENCE   ❑
     GROWING THE BUSINESS   ❑
     DEVELOPING SELF   ❑

Legal Research and Analysis entails the ability to conduct legal research using appropriate journals, texts, documents, etc., and to analyze a legal problem.

1.   PERFORMS ACCURATE RESEARCH:

- Performs the research requested and is able to locate the appropriate "on-point" authority or information to solve the problem presented
- Is familiar with and comfortable using basic legal research tools, including books and computerized research tools.
- Updates and checks validity of authority and extends authority and information to find additional materials.
- Performs analyses that are clear and legally supportable.
- Uses appropriate level of effort for the task (i.e., performs the appropriate amount of research based on partner and case needs).

2.   TAKES INITIATIVE TO PERFORM COMPREHENSIVE RESEARCH:

- When appropriate, aggressively looks for and locates the most helpful authority, even when this entails going beyond the original assignment.

- Uses research to redefine or narrow the research requested and locates useful authority or information, even if not directly on point.

- Analogizes to other types of legal problems to find helpful authority and information.
- Performs all types of legal and factual research using tools including statutory, legislative, regulatory, international, and obscure resources as necessary.
- Performs research that is thorough, creative and reflects in-depth analysis.
- Performing legal research proficiently—especially with computerized research tools—in a cost-effective manner.

3.   **RESEARCH STRATEGIST:**
- Approaches legal problems on many different levels; can locate useful authority or information even on difficult issues, and performs analyses that result in novel or creative solutions.
- Evaluates research results and identifies additional research needs that may not be readily apparent.

4.   **DEFICIENT**

- Does not demonstrate basic competency

5.   **NON-APPLICABLE**

- Have not had opportunity to demonstrate competency and/or competency does not apply to practice or position.

Associate:

_____

You selected level _____.

Please provide specific examples and explanations to support the level you selected. If you do not provide support, the Evaluation Committee may have difficulty in utilizing your review.

Competency Czar

This is a typical page found on Howrey U. Martha Gooding serves as a business development competency czar and has provided the material in this section to help associates master this competency. Use this model to help formulate your own online resources.

Competency Czar Resource Identification Form

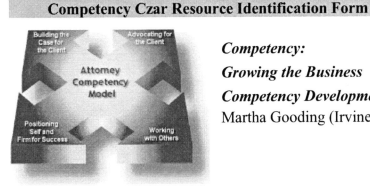

Competency:
Growing the Business
Competency Development Czar:
Martha Gooding (Irvine)

Definition:

Growing the Business entails actively promoting business development through marketing, identifying business opportunities, and participating in or leading activities that result in generating new business—either in terms of immediate or longer-term sales. This includes working to favorably position Howrey in the marketplace—including making presentations and writing papers, articles, etc. It also includes working to build or maintain relationships or networks of contacts with people who may help to develop new or additional business.

Someone with this competency demonstrates the following behaviors:

1. **Identifies Opportunities to Promote Howrey:**

   - Promotes Howrey and what Howrey does in daily interactions with legal community, summer associates, potential clients, and current clients.
   - Remains alert to opportunities to expand business with existing clients or develop new business.
   - Identifies and uses opportunities to meet new people and develop new contacts.

2. **Participates in Business Development Activities:**

   - Identifies opportunities for follow-on business.
   - Spots and exploits opportunities to develop new business or client relationships.
   - Establishes a network of contacts in the business and legal communities.
   - Writes proposal sections.
   - Conducts legal research, prepares articles, and prepares presentations to be presented to the legal community.
   - Establishes networks and develops relationships with more senior attorneys to participate in an existing client relationship.

3. **Plays a Significant Role in Successful Business Development Activities:**

   - Takes action to expand business with existing clients and develop new business.
   - Makes conference presentations to promote Howrey and develop new business.
   - Shows persistence and resilience in working to build business opportunities.
   - Builds and maintains strategic relationships with an eye toward the future development of those relationships into business opportunities.

4. **Plays a Lead Role in Successful Business Development Activities:**

   - Closes deals for new cases or client relationships.
   - Builds long-term opportunities with clients.
   - Continuously broadens and maintains a wide network of relationships and uses established relationships to get new business for the firm.
   - Shares existing client relationships with other partners and associates for cross-selling and other purposes.

Tips for Development

Personal Tips and Stories: Q & A with Martha Gooding

Why do you think this is an important competency at Howrey?

At the macro level, "growing the business" is what keeps Howrey in business. It's what allows this firm to grow, thrive, and prosper. That, in turn, creates opportunities for all of us as individuals.

At the micro level, business development is good for your career. It enhances your skills and your value as a lawyer. It is also personally satisfying to bring clients to the firm or to have someone refer business to you—telling their friends or colleagues that you are the lawyer they need to help solve their problems.

The bottom line is: if you want to be an owner of a business—and in our business that means being a partner—you have to think and act like an owner. Growing the business is the job of every one of us. One of the biggest mistakes young associates make is thinking that growing the business is something that only partners are supposed to do. As a practical matter, young lawyers are not likely—and are not expected—to bring in $100 million cases (although nothing is impossible!). But they are expected to network, to develop and nurture contacts, to prepare (or assist in preparing) articles and presentations and the like—all from day one.

Do you have any fundamental words of wisdom or philosophies on how to be successful in this competency?

- *Do great work.* It's important to realize that everything you do for a client is business development. If the client is happy with you and your work, more work will follow. You don't have to be dealing with the general counsel for that to be true. You may be dealing with associate counsel or the business people; they can make (or influence) decisions on hiring counsel, too.
- *Be yourself.* Watch and learn from others, but find a style and an approach to business development that is comfortable for you.
- *Be proactive.* Do not wait for opportunities to come to you. Search out, find, and create your own opportunities.
- *Think broadly about potential sources of business.* Young lawyers sometimes think they can't develop business because they don't know any general counsel. If you have fallen into that mindset, you need to expand your thinking. For example, some of your law school classmates may have in-house positions right now. Law is a mobile profession; lawyers you know who are now working in a firm may change firms or go in-house. People you know through your community (e.g., your homeowners' association, your children's school) are potential sources of business. Other lawyers are great referral sources, e.g., lawyers for co-defendants, lawyers you meet through bar activities. I've even had opposing counsel refer business to me.
- *Be patient.* Business development is inherently long term. Don't get discouraged.
- *Follow-up, follow-up, follow-up.* It is critical to constantly be thinking of how to follow up on and not to lose contacts. Business development is all

about getting your name in front of people and building and nurturing strategic relationships. Keep a thorough database of your contacts and stay in touch with them. Don't let good contacts slip away.

How do you build strategic, long-term relationships with current or potential clients?

Make your business relationships personal. That means taking time to talk—and, especially, to *listen*—to your contacts. If you have relationships with in-house counsel, make the effort to get to know them on a personal level. If your contact lives locally, find ways to interact socially...and that requires knowing enough about them to know if they would love to accompany you to a baseball game or would prefer an evening at the symphony. If your contact lives out of state, consider calling or e-mailing them just to stay in touch, or arrange to see them if you are in town. If you know they have a particular interest, hobby, or legal concern of specialty and you see an interesting article on it, send it to them with a personal note letting them know you are thinking about them. The firm periodically issues "Client Alerts" on important legal developments; I selectively send them to clients or contacts I think will be interested in or affected by the legal development.

Knowing that "what goes around comes around," I like to make referrals to other lawyers whenever appropriate. If you send business to a lawyer friend or colleague, he or she will probably look for ways to reciprocate. It is not uncommon for our colleagues at Howrey to circulate e-mails looking for a legal referral in another state. If I know someone who would be a possible referral, I don't just give their name to my Howrey colleague. I call the potential referral; tell them one of my partners is looking for a referral; and suggest that I would like to submit their name for consideration. Even if they don't get the business, they know I am trying to send them some business, and will likely keep me in mind next time they need to make a referral.

Sometimes I use referral opportunities as an opportunity to contact an in-house lawyer with whom I have (or am cultivating) a relationship. For example: Someone at Howrey needed a referral to an environmental lawyer in Seattle. I didn't know anyone. But I know an in-house lawyer (from whom I would like to get business) who used to work in the GC's office of a company that I believed had a lot of environmental issues. So I called my contact, told him I was looking for a referral to an environmental lawyer in Seattle, and asked if he could recommend anyone based on his experience in the area. He was flattered that I asked him, and whether or not he knew of someone, it gave me an opportunity to touch base with him, talk a bit about what he was doing, and remind him I'm out there.

Finally, really pay attention. Read about your clients and what is happening in their business and in their industry. Chat with them about their business; find out what's causing them headaches. Let them know you are interested.

You may identify a selling—or cross-selling—opportunity just by listening to what's on their mind.

On-the-Job Developmental Activities and Tips

- It is never too early in your career to begin to think about—and act on—ideas for developing business. Find a style and approach to business development that is comfortable for you.

- Actively participate in professional associations and/or social or community events to build your network of contacts. Think strategically about what organizations you become active in. As an example, get involved in a bar association or a trade association. It's a wonderful source for networking. But just being a member and going to a meeting once a year is not enough; you must be active. The people who get really involved in these organizations move up in the organization—and the more you move up, the more visible you are. Remember, however, that if you take on a task or project for the organization, you must do it, do it on time, and do it well. Part of the reason to be involved in the organization is to network and give people confidence that you can be trusted to handle their legal work; you must show them that you can be trusted to follow through on the organization's work first.

- Follow-up with your contacts on a regular basis. That means, "No random acts of lunch!" Find or create ways to keep your name (and Howrey's) before your contacts. Send them a *Client Alert* or an article of interest. Look for ways you can give value to your client or prospective client.

- Cultivate contacts at all levels; do not assume that only the general counsel makes hiring decisions. Also, don't put all your eggs in one basket. There's a lot of mobility in this business—you may have a great contact at Company X, but that person could always leave that company or even leave the business.

- Look for opportunities to speak or write—get your name out there. You'd be surprised how many organizations publish newsletters and are crying for good submissions.

- Talk with your fellow attorneys to identify ways that you can collaborate. Think beyond the immediate group of people you work with, and even beyond your practice area.

- Think about whether a memo or a brief you have written—or an interesting new case just decided—can be turned into an article. Then do it, before someone else publishes on it.

- Observe what partners who are successful at developing business do. Ask them questions about how they do it.

- Build a strong understanding of your client's industry and business.

- Really listen to your client. Ask them questions. Learning about their business and the issues they are facing may help you spot appropriate opportunities for cross-selling or for new business. It also makes you a more valuable counselor.

- Building rapport is critical, and that means getting to know your client as a person.

- When talking with a (prospective) client, do your homework. Ask questions that show preparation and insightful thinking. Think about questions ahead of time.

- Find opportunities (including outside of work) to make presentations. This will help you to become more confident and more competent when presenting to a variety of audiences.

  o Before making a presentation, rehearse! If you are presenting with a team, rehearse together; you need to look and sound like a cohesive, coordinated team.

  o Learn as much as you can about your client or audience before you make a presentation: Who are they? What are their needs? What will resonate with them?

  o When delivering a presentation, make it dynamic—get the audience involved, tell a personal story, make them laugh. The mood and tone that you create will have a strong impact on the audience.

- Remember that resilience is critical. You have to be able to bounce back from rejection. Business development is a long-term effort. Be patient.

- Invest in yourself and be proactive in your own development. If you feel there are skills you need to build, be proactive in getting the coaching or training you need, even if you must do it on your own time or on your own dime.

Developmental Opportunities to Seek Out (e.g., Pro Bono Cases, Firm Activities)

Satisfied clients translate into more business and potential referrals. Every case you work on is an opportunity to sell yourself (and Howrey). Be responsive and accessible. Make each client feel that it is your only client and that you have nothing more important to do than help that client.

Seek out opportunities to help put together a presentation for a client, prospective client, or professional organization. Even if you do not have a role in the actual delivery of the presentation, you will benefit from the experience of working with others to put the presentation together. In addition, ask to be present when the presentation is delivered, so that you can see how it's done and learn.

Volunteer to write an article—on your own or with others.

Self-Paced and E-Learning Courses

There are several short classes that you can participate in online and at a time convenient to you. Howrey has access to the following courses:

- Making a Presentation
- Giving and Receiving Feedback

Reading and Audio/Visual Material

Articles:

- Robinson, Ginger. *How to Apply the Characteristics of a Great Rainmaker to Your Practice*

- Kohn, Robert. *The Fundamental Principles of Rainmaking.* California Young Lawyers Association—Employment Resource Guide—a publication of the State Bar of California.

- Kohn, Lawrence and Kohn, Robert. *Joining the Big Leagues: Break the Entry Barriers to Rainmaking.* Law Practice, March 2004, pp. 38-39.

- Kohn, Robert and Kohn, Lawrence. *Doing Business with Friends.* The Bottom Line (Official Publication of the State Bar of California, Law Practice Management and Technology Section), February 2002.

- Kohn, Lawrence and Kohn, Robert. *10 Counter-Intuitive Tips for "Working a Room."* The Monitor, Vol 17 (6), Nov/Dec 2002.

- Kohn, Robert, and Kohn, Lawrence. *Following Up After the Lunch.* The Bottom Line, April 2001.

- Kohn, Robert, and Kohn, Lawrence. *Promoting Your Practice Through Non-Profit Organizations.* The Bottom Line, June 2002.

- Zeughauser, Peter D. *Making Partner—Making Rain.* 1998. (First published as *Getting Business—It's the Vision Thing* in Legal Times, January 19, 1998.)

- Piatt, Pearl. *Law Firms Find Associates Can Make Rain, Too.* Los Angeles Daily Journal, July 14, 1997.

Live Seminars

There are a number of seminars that can help you improve in areas related to this competency. Some of these seminars are available in-house. Others may be available outside the firm, but in your area. For example, presentations related to this competency will be included in the following in-house seminars:

- Howrey Academies, especially the Advanced Associate Academy

Individual Development Plan Example

After an associate receives his or her performance evaluation, he or she develops an individual development plan, focusing on two or three competencies to work on for the year.

Individual Development Plan

Instructions: Complete the following by listing three developmental goals based on your performance evaluation. Then, set up a time to discuss the plan with your local training partner. Submit your completed form on the performance evaluation system so it can be included in your file next evaluation period.

Sample Development Goal	Action Plan	Timing/Success metric	Completion
1. Oral Advocacy— -Improve my ability to: -Articulate arguments and ideas in an understandable fashion -Present arguments and ideas in a persuasive manner -Handle a court hearing	Take on a pro bono case with courtroom opportunities	Spring 2005 Completed pro bono case that resulted in successful advocating before a judge	__Not completed __Partially completed __Fully completed
2. Project and Case Management—improve my ability to: -Prioritize tasks -Manage meetings well; state agenda and objectives clearly -Plan and anticipate to ensure completion of specific projects in a timely and efficient manner	Complete e-learning courses on Project Management and Keeping Teams on Target. Ask for feedback from partner and peers on my effectiveness	Complete courses by February 2005. Improved skills as noted by partner and peers.	__Not completed __Partially completed __Fully completed

Section to be submitted through the performance evaluation system

Development Goal	Action Plan	Timing/Success metric	Completion
1.			__Not completed __Partially completed __Fully completed
2.			__Not completed __Partially completed __Fully completed
3.			__Not completed __Partially completed __Fully completed

Pro Bono Closure Form

This form is completed at the close of every pro bono case. The information gleaned from this report helps the pro bono committee choose future cases that will help associates master competencies. It also helps the associates and reviewing partners track specific experiences at evaluation time.

PRO BONO CLOSURE FORM

INSTRUCTIONS: Please provide the following information to facilitate the firm's tracking of pro bono matters.

CLIENT INFORMATION

1. File/Matter Number: 2. Client Name:

MATTER INFORMATION

3. Matter Description: 4. Resolution of Case:

CLOSURE INFORMATION

5. Date Acctg. Notified to Close
   Billing Number:

6. Date Attorney Sent
   Closure Letter:

(Attach copy to this form.)

7.

_____

Attorney signature   **Date**

_____

Public Service Counsel

---

8. Please describe the professional experience of the attorneys on the case:

Depositions taken ❑ Yes ❑ No
Number of depositions _____
Name(s) of attorney(s) who took depositions:

_____

Depositions defended ❑ Yes ❑ No
Number of depositions _____
Name(s) of attorney(s) who defended depositions:

Document production ❑ Yes ❑ No
Expert report ❑ Yes ❑ No
Expert deposition taken ❑ Yes ❑ No
Name(s) of attorney(s) who took deposition

_____

Expert deposition defended ❑ Yes ❑ No
Name(s) of attorney(s) who defended deposition

_____

Motion to dismiss filed ❑ Yes ❑ No
Motion to dismiss opposed ❑ Yes ❑ No
Motion for summary judgment filed ❑ Yes ❑ No
Motion for summary judgment opposed ❑ Yes ❑ No
Motions hearing(s) (list all) _____
Name(s) of attorney(s) who argued motion(s):

_____

Jury trial ❑ Yes ❑ No
How many days _____
Name(s) of attorney(s) who had witnesses or argued at trial:

_____

Bench trial ❑ Yes ❑ No
How many days _____
Name(s) of attorney(s) who had witnesses or argued at trial:

_____

Appellate brief filed ❑ Yes ❑ No
Appellate argument ❑ Yes ❑ No
Name(s) of attorney(s) who argued:

_____

Settlement conference ❑ Yes ❑ No

Associate Workload Report

This report can be used to track associate assignments and the competencies that are related to those assignments.

Associate Name: _____

Two-Week Period: _____

ASSOCIATE WORKLOAD REPORT FORM
E-mail to _____ by 2:00 p.m., Monday

Estimated Workload (including pro bono)

Week of _____	On target for X/hours annually	On target for X/hours annually	On target for X/hours annually
	Light ☐	Medium ☐	Heavy ☐
Week of _____	☐	☐	☐

What were your billable (including approved pro bono) hours last week?
What were your billable (including approved pro bono) hours last month?
Were your hours last week affected by vacation or other events?

On which client are you principally working, and for which partners?

Other comments?

What is your availability for new assignments?

Are you looking for certain types of assignments or competency development? (Which?)

Building the Case for the Client
___Legal Research and Analysis
___Factual Development and
   Investigation
___Mastery of Substantive and
   Procedural Law
___Creative Problem Solving

Advocating for the Client
___Written Advocacy
___Oral Advocacy
___Negotiation Skills
___Trial and Courtroom Skills

Positioning Firm for Success
___Client Service and Communication
___Growing the Business

Working with Others
___Project/Case Management
___Leadership

(If you want the staffing committee to actively look for assignments on your behalf, please contact one of the committee representatives (contact the point person listed at the top if you are unsure of your committee representative).)

	Short-Term/Emergency	
No Availability	Assignment Only	Long-Term Assignments
☐	☐	☐
	% of time available	% of time available to take on long term

Bibliography

Abbott, Ida O. *Lawyers' Professional Development: The Legal Employer's Comprehensive Guide.* Washington, DC: NALP, 2002.

Boyatzis, Richard. *Resonant Leadership.* Boston: Harvard Business School Press, 2005.

Bridges, William. *Managing Transitions: Making the Most of Change.* New York: Addison-Wesley Publishing Company, 1991.

Collins, Jim. *Good to Great.* New York: HarperCollins, 2001.

Gladwell, Malcolm. *The Tipping Point.* New York: Back Bay Books, 2000.

Gluckman, Steve. "Using Technology to Enable Competency Management." Chief Learning Officer, December 2005.

Kotter, John P. and Heskett, James L. *Corporate Culture and Performance.* New York: The Free Press, 1992.

Senge, Peter. *The Fifth Discipline.* New York: Doubleday Currency, 1990.

Snider, Debra. *The Productive Culture Blueprint for Corporate Law Departments and Their Outside Counsel.* American Bar Association Career Resource Center, 2003.

Index

A

C

tactics, 4, 15

Professional development plans, 2, 34, 59, 71

Project manager, 32

R

Rating errors and biases, 61

Reaction to evaluation process, 73

Reaction to training, 72

Recruiting, 12, 62, 88-89

    budget, 12, 42

    competency model as foundation for, 8

    processes, 70

Recruiting Committee, 62

Regional and international offices, 45

Ripley, Rick, 9

Rollout of the model, 62-63

    checklist, 63

    reaction to rollout, 71

Rushton, Terre, 41, 44

Ruyak, Robert F., iii, vii

S

Self-evaluations, 59

Senge, Peter, 38, 121

Senior Associate Academy, 49

Seyfarth Shaw, LLP, 4-5

Skill development, 21, 46

Skill levels, 29

Snider, Debra, 38, 121

Soft skills, 1, 13, 48-49

    and Center for Management and Leadership, 54

Stacy, Caren Ulrich, 5

    see Arnold & Porter LLP

Staff people, 22

Strategic drivers, 24

    strategic management plans, 2